T0116535

YOUNG WARRIOR'S
DEVOTIONAL COLORING BOOK

ELDER MARION MINORS

BALBOA.PRESS

A DIVISION OF HAY HOUSE

This book is a work of non-fiction. Unless otherwise noted, the author and the publisher make no explicit guarantees as to the accuracy of the information contained in this book and in some cases, names of people and places have been altered to protect their privacy.

Balboa Press books may be ordered through booksellers or by contacting:

Balboa Press
A Division of Hay House
1663 Liberty Drive
Bloomington, IN 47403
www.balboapress.com
844-682-1282

Because of the dynamic nature of the Internet, any web addresses or links contained in this book may have changed since publication and may no longer be valid. The views expressed in this work are solely those of the author and do not necessarily reflect the views of the publisher, and the publisher hereby disclaims any responsibility for them.

The author of this book does not dispense medical advice or prescribe the use of any technique as a form of treatment for physical, emotional, or medical problems without the advice of a physician, either directly or indirectly. The intent of the author is only to offer information of a general nature to help you in your quest for emotional and spiritual well-being. In the event you use any of the information in this book for yourself, which is your constitutional right, the author and the publisher assume no responsibility for your actions.

Any people depicted in stock imagery provided by Getty Images are models, and such images are being used for illustrative purposes only. Certain stock imagery © Getty Images.

Scriptures quoted from the International Children's Bible®, copyright ©1986, 1988, 1999, 2015 by Tommy Nelson. Used by permission.

Interior Image Credit: Skye Minors

Print information available on the last page.

ISBN: 979-8-7652-3448-8 (sc)
ISBN: 979-8-7652-3450-1 (hc)
ISBN: 979-8-7652-3449-5 (e)

Balboa Press rev. date: 10/26/2022

CONTENTS

Follow The Rules!

*"Serve only the Lord your God. Respect
Him. Keep His commands and obey Him.
Serve Him and be loyal to Him."*
—*Deuteronomy 13:4*

We all love our parents and want to do everything that pleases them to show how much we love them. In the same way, when we follow God's rules, we show God how much we love Him.

Gabriella (everyone called her Gabby) was so excited. She was going to Windy Woods Summer Camp this year. She had not been able to go last year, because she was too young. Now, Gabby had turned eight, and she was ready.

Mom told her that at the camp, she would be able to learn so many new things—things like fishing, arts and crafts, archery (which is how to use a bow and arrow), and new songs. Most of all, she would meet new people and make new friends.

It was Monday morning, the day camp started. Gabby was up early. She brushed her teeth and got dressed in her new camp T-shirt. It had "Welcome to Windy Woods Summer Camp" printed on the front.

She felt so proud when she looked in the mirror. Her blue jeans looked especially nice with her camp shirt.

She ran downstairs, ate—well, actually, she gulped up her pancakes—and ran to the door, saying, "Come on, Mom and Dad. I am ready to go."

But Mom answered, "Oh, Gabby, we still have at least an hour before we have to go. Just relax."

Gabby pushed her suitcase, her sleeping bag, and Mr. Purple Bear closer to the door. She had to make sure Mr. Purple Bear was ready because she just could not go to camp without him. You see, Grandma Foster had given him to her a long time ago, and she just loved him so much.

After about an hour, Mom said, "It's time to go, Gabby. Dad is putting all of your things in the car now."

Gabby jumped up off the couch and ran out the door. She was finally on her way to camp.

They drove to the school parking lot, where there were buses waiting to take all the kids to camp. She kissed Mom and Dad goodbye and ran to get on the bus.

What a wonderful time she had on the bus. Everyone on the bus sang songs Gabby had not heard before—songs like "Row, Row, Row Your Boat"; "B-I-N-G-O"; "On Top of Spaghetti"; and so many more.

When the buses finally arrived at the camp, everyone went to the camp hall. A woman and man were there, and the woman said, "Excuse me, everyone! Can I have your attention, please? My name is Mrs. Frank, and this is my husband, Mr. Frank. We are the leaders of this camp. Please settle down so I can give you the number of the cabin you will be staying in. There will be four children and one counselor in each one."

She called out the names and numbers of each cabin. Gabby was in cabin number four, along with Ms. Wells, the counselor; Jessica; Ryanna; and Kim. Mrs. Frank then called up each counselor to the front so the children could follow them to their cabins.

When the girls got to the cabin, Ms. Wells introduced herself and asked the girls to each say something about themselves.

Jessica said, "I like to sing."

Ryanna said, "I love to meet new people."

Kim said, "I love to play games."

Then Gabby said, "I am so excited to be here."

Ms. Wells said, "I am so glad that you are here and in my cabin. I hope we all can have a wonderful time as we learn more about each other. But right now, I must let you know what the camp rules are. If you follow these rules, I know we all will enjoy our stay at Windy Woods Camp."

She continued, "Rule number one, you must be kind to each other; number two, you must treat others as you want them to treat you; number three, you must be obedient to your counselor; and finally, number four, you must follow all of these rules."

Gabby was ready to follow the rules because she already knew about them. She said to herself, "These rules are just like the rules in the Bible that my Sunday school taught." She knew she would even have a wonderful time obeying the rules because she followed these rules all the time at home and in school.

You know, Gabby was right; these rules are in the Bible. Let me show you.

Rule #1: You must be kind to each other.

Ephesians 4:32: "Be kind and loving to each other."

Rule #2: You must treat others as you want them to treat you.

Luke 6:31: "Do for other people what you want them to do for you."

Rule #3: You must be obedient to your counselor.

Titus 3:1: "Remind the believers to do these things: to obey their leaders and to do good."

Rule #4: You must follow these rules.

Deuteronomy 13:4: "Serve only the Lord your God. Respect Him. Keep His commands and obey Him. Serve Him and be loyal to Him."

The campers would have a wonderful time at camp if they followed the camp rules.

Do you know you can have a wonderful time every day of your life just by following these same rules?

Rule #1: If you see someone trip and fall, don't laugh. Help them up, and make sure that they are okay. This is showing kindness to others.

Rule #2: When someone in your class hurts you and says they're sorry, you should accept their apology because wouldn't you want them to accept yours?

Rule #3: Teachers are our leaders, so we need to obey their rules.

Rule #4: Following rules is obeying God and showing Him that we love Him.

If we as God's children follow His rules in the Bible, we, too, can be happy every day of our lives.

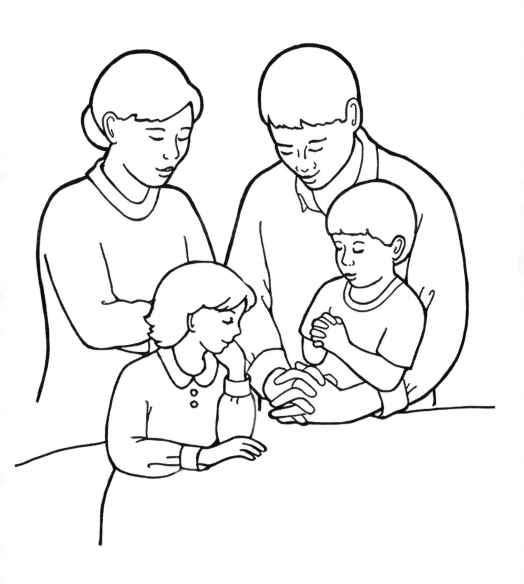

Right on Time

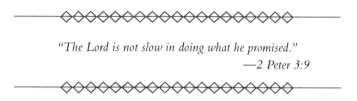

"The Lord is not slow in doing what he promised."
—*2 Peter 3:9*

If God makes a promise, He always keeps it. I remember when I was eleven years old, I was very sick. I was put in the hospital's adult ward because there weren't any beds in the children's ward. It was very scary in the adult ward, and at night, it was even worse. The second night, I woke up in the middle of the night, and this old lady was standing right over my bed. I screamed and she ran off. I prayed and asked God to make room in the children's ward for me because I was so afraid. Even though it seemed like God wasn't going to answer my prayer, I was moved to the children's ward two days later. God promises that if we believe and trust Him when we pray, we will have what we ask for. Matthew 21:22 says, "If you believe, you will get anything you ask for in prayer." Even though it was scary, I had to trust and wait on God.

Sissy was a young girl who loved the Lord and believed in His Word. Her real name was Sisley, but everyone called her Sissy. Sissy and her parents were members of the Greater Temple of God Church. She enjoyed going to church with her parents. Her favorite part of service was the prayer session. Sissy loved the fact that when the adults prayed, they encouraged the young people to pray also.

In so many of their services, when they prayed, people got healed and had their lives changed forever. She remembered one time, a lady came to church in a wheelchair, and when people prayed for her, she was healed and began to walk. There were many miracles like this that happened in the Greater Temple of God Church.

Her parents were people who prayed to God all the time. Before Dad left for work and Sissy left for school, the family would get together and pray. Also, before they went to bed every night, they prayed together. They read the Bible every day and loved to serve the Lord.

One day when Sissy and Mom were at the mall eating lunch, an older lady sat at a table near to them. She looked really sad and lonely, so Mom said hello and asked her, "Is everything okay?"

She replied, "I am fine, but sometimes, I really feel so lonely. You see, my family lives far away from me, and I don't get to see them often."

"That's too bad," Mom answered, "but I know someone who will always be with you so you don't feel alone."

"Really?" the woman replied. "Who is it, and where can I find them?" she asked. Mom told her about Jesus and how much He loved her.

Do you know that right there in the mall, the woman asked Jesus to come into her life? She was so happy and said, "Oh, I feel so much better. Thank you, and I thank Jesus for loving me so much."

Sissy was not surprised, because this happened all the time. Mom loved God so much that she always shared His love with others.

One Friday evening, when Dad came home, he did not look very happy. You see, the company he worked for was not making much money, so his paycheck had been cut about a month ago. He had less money, so not all the bills were getting paid. But the family kept praying and believed God would make a way.

Unfortunately, one of the people the family owed money to wanted them to pay right away. They had sent Dad a letter to say the money would have to be paid by the next Friday, which was only one week away.

Dad, Mom, and Sissy believed in John 15:7, which says, "Remain in me and follow my teachings. If you do this, then you can ask for anything you want, and it will be given to you." Remember that they had seen so many miracles happen in people's lives. Now, they needed one, and they believed it would happen for them.

They prayed, "Dear God, we know You love us, and we love You. We try our best to please You. Thank You for always being faithful and blessing us and for all the miracles You have done in our lives. We are asking You to bless us again with another miracle. We need money to pay off this bill. We thank You, Lord, because we believe You and know You will do this for us. In Jesus's name, amen!" Each day, as they always did, they prayed as a family.

Well, Friday came, and they had not yet received the money needed, but they continued to believe God. Even by the time Sissy came home from school that afternoon, they had not received the answer to their prayer. Sissy and Mom took time to pray, and they began to thank God for the money they needed.

About an hour later, the phone rang. It was Dad. Mom answered, and Sissy was sitting next to her, anxiously waiting to hear what was going on.

Mom had such a big smile on her face when she put down the phone. She shouted out, "Praise the Lord! God, You are so faithful. Thank You, Jesus."

Immediately, Mom and Sissy danced around the house and were so happy. They had received their miracle.

Dad explained that a friend of his whom he had not seen for a long time called him. The friend apologized to Dad because a few years ago, Dad had loaned him some money, but he had never paid it back. The friend said, "I have the money, and I am on my way to your office to pay you." It was exactly the amount of money Dad needed to pay the bill.

When Dad got home that night, the family thanked God and praised Him for His faithfulness. Dad said, "We must remember what 2 Peter 3:8 says. The Lord is not slow in doing what He promised. He has perfect timing: never early, never late. God is never in a hurry, but He is *always on time*."

When you pray, asking God for something, always remember God is never early and never late; He is always on time with the answer. We can be like Sissy's family and believe God is faithful to His promises.

Is there a miracle that your family needs? Write down your prayer to God, and you can believe God to answer at just the right time.

Forgiveness

*"If you don't forgive the wrongs of others,
then your Father in heaven will not
forgive the wrong things you do."*
—*Matthew 6:15*

Do you know that when someone hurts you, you have to forgive them 490 times? In Matthew 18:21–22, Peter asks Jesus, "How many times should I forgive someone?"

Jesus answers, "Seventy times seven."

Wow! That's a lot of forgiveness. But if we want God to forgive us, we need to forgive others.

Kerry and Jenny were best friends. They had become friends when they were in the first grade and had been friends ever since. Kerry and Jenny did everything together—shop, play games, play sports—and they were even in the same class. Sometimes, they even dressed alike.

At the beginning of class one day, the teacher announced that the election for class president would begin the next day. Kerry was so excited because she had always wanted to be class president. Believe it or not, so had Jenny. As best friends, they decided they could both run, and whoever won, the other would be OK with it.

Kerry won, and she was so happy the day it was announced. But it wasn't a happy day for Jenny. She was so disappointed she began to hate the fact that Kerry won. She became so angry that she asked Kerry to let her be class president instead.

Kerry was shocked and couldn't believe it. She said to Jenny, "I thought you were my best friend, and we decided regardless of who won, we would be okay. Why are you asking me that?"

Jenny became even angrier and replied, "But I would be a better class president than you ever could be. It should be me. Let me be class president, or I will never speak to you again. I hate you." And then she ran out of the classroom.

Over the next few weeks, Kerry tried to speak with Jenny, but she would not answer her phone calls or her text messages.

At first, Kerry felt sad, but after a while, she said to herself, "Well, if Jenny doesn't want to be friends with me anymore, that's fine. I don't want to be friends with her either. I will be the best class president ever."

Weeks went by, but Kerry really wasn't happy. She really missed her best friend, and Jenny still wasn't speaking to her. One day after school, when she got home, Dad noticed how sad she was and asked her, "What's wrong, Kerry? Why do you look so sad?"

Kerry told Dad the whole story, then asked him, "What should I do? I miss her, but she was so mean to me."

He told her something that she couldn't believe. He said, "You have to forgive her so you two can be friends again."

"What?" Kerry said. "Why do I have to forgive her? She was mean to me."

Dad told her what the Bible tells us in Matthew 6:15, which is this: "If you don't forgive the wrongs of others, then your Father in heaven will not forgive the wrong things you do." He continued, "When we asked Jesus to come into our hearts and forgive us of all the wrong things we did, He forgave us, didn't He?"

Kerry said yes.

"So," Dad said, "Jesus wants us to also forgive people who do wrong things to us. After Jesus forgave you, didn't you feel much better?" he asked.

"Yes, I really did feel much better," Kerry answered. "Okay, I see what you mean. If I forgive Jenny, she will feel better, and so will I."

"Absolutely," Dad said, "and not only that, but Jesus will also be pleased with you."

Kerry knew how hard it would be to forgive Jenny, so she asked Dad to pray with her. He prayed, "Dear Jesus, give Kerry the strength to forgive Jenny, and help her know you are always with her. Amen." Even though Kerry knew that it would be hard to forgive, she had to because she wanted to obey God's Word.

The next day, when she saw Jenny, Kerry wanted to run up to her and forgive her, but she couldn't. It was harder than she had thought. But she continued to ask Jesus to help her.

A few days later, she stopped Jenny and asked to talk. Kerry said, "Jenny, you have always been my best friend. Can you forgive me for hurting your feelings?"

Jenny was really surprised, and she answered, "Oh, Kerry, thank you, but I should be the one asking you to forgive me. I am so sorry for the way I acted. It was terrible, and no one should treat their best friend like that. Can you forgive me?"

Both girls started crying, then hugged and forgave each other. The best friends were together again, and they were very happy.

It is not always easy to forgive when someone hurts you, but as Kerry and Jenny learned, you have to forgive because if you don't, then Jesus won't forgive you. When you forgive, not only are you and the other person happy, but Jesus is also pleased and happy with you.

Can you think of an example when you practiced forgiveness or when someone forgave you? How did it make you feel? Is there anyone who needs your forgiveness? Ask God to help you.

Red Robin

*"He was wounded for the wrong things we did.
He was crushed for the evil things we did. The
punishment, which made us well, was given to Him.
And we are healed because of His wounds."*
—Isaiah 53:5

John 14:14 says, "If you ask me for anything in my name, I will do it." Here, Jesus was saying that if we ask for anything—even for healing— and believe, He will do it.

Every morning in Tinderville, neighbors would hear the lovely sound of a bird singing. It was Red Robin. All her neighbors loved to hear her sing because it made them very happy. If anyone woke up not feeling well, the sound of Red Robin's singing would make them feel better. It would cheer them up!

One morning, when Red Robin's neighbor Blue Bird woke up, he couldn't believe it; he didn't hear any singing. He waited for a moment. He thought maybe something was wrong with his hearing, so he called Yellow Bird.

"Good morning, Yellow Bird," he said. "Do you hear Red Robin singing?"

"No, as a matter of fact, I don't," she answered.

Now, Blue Bird started to worry. So they both decided to go check on Red Robin.

When they got to Red Robin's house, they knocked on the door and waited for her to welcome them in, but they didn't hear anything. They knocked about three or four times, waited, and then decided to go in. They opened the door, and Red Robin was sitting on the couch.

"What's the matter?" Blue Bird asked.

Red Robin looked at him, and she couldn't even speak. She wrote on a piece of paper that she had lost her voice and the doctor wasn't sure when it would come back. Her neighbors were shocked and so upset to think that they would not hear her beautiful singing anymore. They decided to call a meeting with all the neighbors to discuss the situation.

At the beginning, the neighbors discussed the situation for a long time, but no one came up with a solution until Blue Bird's son, Calen, raised his hand and said, "I know what we can do."

"Tell us," everyone answered.

Calen replied, "I remember when my grandfather was sick, my grandmother and some friends prayed for him, and a few days later, he was fine. When they finished praying, my grandmother said, 'By Jesus's stripes, you are healed.' Maybe we could pray for Red Robin so she can get better and be healed too."

The neighbors all agreed that this was a wonderful idea.

The next morning, they all met at Red Robin's house to pray for her. They asked Blue Bird to pray. He said, "Jesus, we thank You for this opportunity to pray for Red Robin. The Bible says in Isaiah 53:5, 'He was wounded for the wrong things we did. He was crushed for the evil things we did. The punishment, which made us well, was given to him. And we are healed because of his wounds.' So we are believing Your Word, God, and ask You to heal Red Robin so we can hear that beautiful voice again. Also, the Bible says in John 14:14, 'If you ask Me for anything in My name, I will do it.' We are asking in Your name, Jesus, and we thank You for healing Red Robin and making her well."

Then all the neighbors said, "Amen!"

The next morning, when everyone woke up, they still didn't hear Red Robin's beautiful voice, but they continued to believe that Jesus would make her well.

A few mornings later, there was so much laughing and excitement because they all heard Red Robin's beautiful voice. Her songs sounded even more wonderful. She was singing again!

The Bible says in Mark 11:24, "I tell you to ask for things in prayer. And if you believe that you have received those things, then they will be yours."

This is what happened with Red Robin's neighbors. They believed the Word of God, and their friend was healed.

Is anyone who you know sick? Write your prayer for them using the scripture verse in Isaiah 53:5.

Wonderfully Made

*"I praise You because You made me in an
amazing and wonderful way. What You have
done is wonderful. I know this very well."*
—Psalm 139:14

God made us all beautiful in His image. I didn't always believe this.
For as long as I can remember, I have been very skinny. My family and
friends would always tease me and call me names like Sticks in a Paper
Bag, Chopsticks, Bone, or Bony Legs. I was very hurt by these names
and didn't like myself very much.

But one day, my mother called me, gave me a big hug, and said,
"You are fearfully and wonderfully made by God." She said I needed
to accept how God had made me and be thankful in all things. She also
reminded me that there were people in the world who didn't have any
legs and would love to even have skinny ones. I began to thank God
for my skinny legs and became proud of who He made me.

One day, someone shouted, "Hey, look at Freckle Face!"

But the answer they heard surprised them. That answer was "I
know, I am so grateful to God because I am unique. I love my freckles."

Jolene was the person who said it. She was finally able to say that she loved her freckles. But you know, it wasn't always like this. At one time, she hated her freckles. Let me tell you what happened.

Jolene was born with freckles all over her face. The kids in school always teased her about them. When she got home from school, she would usually go right to her room and cry. It was really bad. This went on for quite some time. Over the school year, she stopped hanging around the other students. She would eat lunch alone and even be by herself in the schoolyard.

Her parents knew something was wrong, but every time they asked her, she would tell them everything was fine and not to worry.

One day as Jolene got dressed for school, Mom came into her room and said, "Jolene, you look so beautiful, and that outfit is really nice."

Jolene shouted back, "What, with these disgusting freckles, I am not beautiful at all. I am just ugly."

Mom was so surprised. She didn't know what to say at first, but she answered, "No, sweetheart, you are beautiful, and I love you so much, and God loves you too."

"How could God love an ugly person like me?" Jolene asked.

Mom said, "Come here, sweetheart. I want to talk to you," and they sat down on the bed. "Of course, God loves you, and you know what? He loves those freckles too."

"He does?" Jolene answered because she couldn't imagine God would love her freckles.

Mom continued, "You see, in the Bible, in Psalm 139:14, David says, 'I praise You because You made me in an amazing and wonderful way. What You have done is wonderful. I know this very well.' He was thanking God for how amazing and wonderfully He made him. God gave you those freckles because they are amazing and wonderful and because He loves you. God gave you to Daddy and me as a gift. The Bible says in James 1:17, 'Every good action and every perfect gift is from God.' So that means you are perfect in God's eyes, and it also says in 1 Timothy 4:4, 'Everything that God made is good.' So, my sweetheart, you are amazing, wonderful, perfect, and good because God made you.

"Just like David, you must thank God for those beautiful freckles and that cute face that we love. I know it might be hard to do, but if you keep working at it, it will get easier. The next time someone wants to say something bad about your freckles, I want you to remember that it is only coming from the devil. He is the one who is causing people to be mean to you, and the way to stop him is to thank God because he really doesn't like that. The next time, say, 'I know, I am so grateful to God because I am amazing. I love my freckles.'"

The next day, when someone shouted, "Hey, look at Freckle Face. She looks so ugly," Jolene started to get upset, but she remembered what Mom said. She answered, "I know, I am so grateful to God because I am unique. I love my freckles."

After a while, the other students stopped teasing her, and Jolene realized that not only was she amazing and beautiful, but also in order to stop the enemy, you must use the Word of God.

So whether you have red hair, blue eyes, or dark skin, or you are very tall or very short, it doesn't matter to God, because He loves you very much and He made you amazing and wonderful!

Make a list of some things about yourself that you are teased for and you don't like. Now, make another list of things that God says in His Word about you.

You Gotta Be Kidding

*"Love your enemies. Do good to them and lend to
them without hoping to get anything back. If you do
these things, you will have a great reward. You will be
sons of the Most High God. Yes, because God is kind
even to people who are ungrateful and full of sin."*
—Luke 6:35

If we are children of God, no matter how hard it is, we have to love
our enemies. The wonderful thing is that God gives us the power and
love to do this, and when we do, it pleases Him.

It seemed that all Gina could say when she thought of what she had
learned in Sunday school that morning was "You gotta be kidding."
Even later, after the family had finished Sunday dinner, she had gone
straight to her room. Sitting on her bed, she could only think, *You gotta
be kidding.*

Earlier that morning, in her Sunday school class, Gina's teacher had
read the Bible verse Luke 6:35–36, which says, "Love your enemies. Do
good to them and lend to them without hoping to get anything back. If
you do these things, you will have a great reward. You will be sons of
the Most High God. Yes, because God is kind even to people who are
ungrateful and full of sin. Show mercy just as your father shows mercy."

The teacher had said that because they had the love of Jesus in their hearts, they had to love their enemies. Gina had been so surprised and thought, *How can I love my enemy?*

Just at that moment, Daddy passed by her room and saw her sitting on her bed.

He asked, "Is everything okay, Gina?"

She wasn't ready to talk, so she answered, "Yes, Daddy."

"Okay," he said, "but just know I am here when you are ready to talk."

"Okay," she answered. She continued to sit on her bed, still trying to understand how she could love her enemy. Finally, she decided that she really needed to talk about it, and besides, she needed to know. She jumped off her bed and went down to Daddy, who was in the den.

When she walked in, Daddy said, "So I guess you are ready to talk."

"Yes," Gina answered. "Daddy," she said, "this morning in Sunday school class, the teacher read a scripture about loving your enemies, but I can't understand how anyone can do that."

Daddy sat and listened, and then he said, "Yes, it's a very hard thing to do, but I know someone who did it."

"Really?" Gina answered. "Who?"

"Well," Daddy said, "it was Jesus Himself. You remember the story about when Jesus died on the cross. Before He died, He asked God to forgive all those people who wanted to crucify Him. Remember He died for all our sins because He loved us, and He also showed that love by forgiving His enemies. That is why He commanded us to love our enemies, so we can show them the love of Jesus."

Gina thought for a while. Then she said, "Oh, now I get it, but it's going to be very hard. You see, Daddy, there is an enemy in my classroom that is a bully. He pushes people around and is very mean, but if Jesus wants me to show His love, then I will try."

"Good," Daddy answered. "Do you want me to pray for you so God can give you the strength to do it?"

"Oh, yes, Daddy," Gina said, "definitely."

Then Daddy prayed not only for Gina but also for the enemy in her class and encouraged Gina to pray for him too.

The next day, Gina went to school determined to show love to the enemy, whose name was Craig. Well, the day seemed to be going okay until lunch break, when Craig came up to her and bumped into her, and everything she had in her hand fell to the floor. She was not pleased at all, but she remembered her memory verse and just smiled.

That night, when she said her prayers, she remembered to pray for Craig.

At first, things at school didn't change very much, but she continued to smile and even said to Craig, "God loves you, and so do I." The first time she said it, he stopped and just stared at her.

Then, after a few weeks, she saw a change in Craig. He was not so mean anymore. One day, he came up to her and asked, "Why do you smile and say, 'God loves you, and so do I'? Are you some sort of nut? You would have to be a nut because I have been really mean to you, but you still treat me with kindness. Why?"

Gina replied, "Because I love Jesus, and He wants me to share His love even with my enemies so they can see His love in me."

Craig said, "I could tell there was something different about you. You know, sometimes, I really don't want to be mean, but it just happens."

Gina answered, "Jesus knows your heart, and He can help you to be good. All you have to do is tell Him how sorry you are for doing the mean things. Ask Him to come into your heart, and He will fill you with His love."

You may not have a mean boy like Craig in your class, but you may have someone who tells lies about you. It doesn't matter, because if you belong to Jesus, He wants you to love your enemies so they can see His love in you.

When was the last time that you shared the love of Jesus with someone who was difficult to love?

Standing Ovation

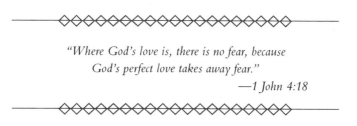

*"Where God's love is, there is no fear, because
God's perfect love takes away fear."*
—1 John 4:18

The Bible says God did not give us a spirit that makes us afraid. He gave us a spirit of power and love and self-control. So He does not want us to be afraid, because He promised never to leave us. It doesn't matter what may happen in our lives; we have to remember He is always with us.

"I can't do it and I won't do it. It's too hard!" screamed Julie, running to her room and slamming the door. She was really upset.

But let's start at the beginning of our story.

It was two weeks before graduation from preschool to first grade. At the end of the school day, the teacher, Miss Fletcher, called all the students around her desk. She said, "Listen, we will have our graduation in only two weeks, so we have to practice for our program. I will pick some of you to sing, and some of you will be speakers. I will let you know tomorrow what everyone will be doing. Have a good day!"

When Julie's mom picked her up, she was so excited and told Mommy what Miss Fletcher said. She really hoped she would be picked to be a speaker.

The next day, Miss Fletcher told everyone what they would be doing for the graduation program, and yes, Julie was a speaker. Can you imagine how excited she was? She told Miss Fletcher that she would really practice hard to learn her lines.

When Mommy picked Julie up from school, she told Mommy the good news. Even on the way home, Julie was practicing her lines. In fact, Mommy had to stop her from practicing so she could eat her supper. She was even practicing in the bathtub.

The next morning at school, Julie ran up to Miss Fletcher and said, "Guess what? I almost know all my lines already. I practiced all night." Miss Fletcher was impressed and told Julie what a great job she was doing. By the end of the first week before graduation, Julie knew all her lines.

Now two days before the program, Miss Fletcher and her class went to the hall and practiced. Everyone did a great job, but Miss Fletcher reminded them that they would have to speak loudly so all the people could hear them clearly.

What! Julie thought. *I didn't know it was going to be in front of a lot of people. I don't know if I can do that.* She didn't feel too well after that. And when Mommy picked her up, she was really not herself.

Mommy asked, "What's the matter, sweetheart? You seem really quiet today."

Julie just shrugged her shoulders and said, "Nothing."

When they arrived home, Julie went right up to her bedroom. Now, Mommy knew something was wrong and called her back downstairs.

When Julie came downstairs, Mommy gave her a big hug and asked again if anything was wrong.

Julie began to cry, and sobbing, she answered, "I don't know what I'm going to do. I really don't know."

"About what?" Mommy asked.

She replied, "I found out today that our graduation is going to be performed in front of a lot of people. I can't be a speaker. I am afraid I might forget my lines or mess up a word. I can't do it and I won't do it. It's too hard."

Julie screamed, ran to her room, and slammed the door. Mommy gently opened the door and gave Julie even more hugs and lots of kisses.

When Julie was calm, Mommy said, "I know who can help you. Listen to me for a minute. Remember a few weeks ago when we were doing our devotions, we read a scripture in the Bible? I think it was 2 Timothy 1:7, and it said, 'God did not give us a spirit that makes us afraid. He gave us a spirit of power and love and self-control.' Do you remember what it means?"

Julie answered, "No."

Mommy continued, "It means that when we asked Jesus to come into our hearts, His Holy Spirit came to be with us to help us obey God. So, the Holy Spirit helps us not to be afraid. He is there to help us be brave, especially when we have to do something that is very hard."

"Oh, now I remember," Julie replied. "We learned that the Holy Spirit is God's spirit who will guide and lead us in the right way and the right thing to do. I did promise Miss Fletcher that I would do a great job, so I have to keep my promise, right?"

"Well, yes," Mommy said, "but also because we know the Holy Spirit is the spirit of God, we know God is with us. We don't have to be afraid. You see, in 1 John 4:18, it says, 'Where God's love is, there is no fear, because God's perfect love takes away fear.' So, because God's love is perfect, it's perfect in us, and that perfect love takes away all fear. The next time that 'mean spirit' of fear wants to come around, you just tell him, 'I will not be afraid, because God's perfect love lives in me, and it takes away all fear.'"

"Wow!" shouted Julie. "I am not afraid anymore, because now I know the perfect love of God lives in me and it takes away all fear. I will do it. I can do it, and I am ready to do it."

On the night of the graduation program, Julie remembered all her lines. She spoke slowly and very loudly so even the people at the back heard her. When she finished, everyone clapped and even gave her a standing ovation.

Julie was so proud of herself and ran backstage to Mommy. She asked Mommy if they could pray and thank God for His perfect love, which had taken away all her fear.

God's perfect love can live inside you too when you ask Jesus to come into your heart. He fills you with His Holy Spirit and His perfect love to take away all your fear.

Is there anything that you are afraid to do or that you feel is too hard? For the next five days, practice speaking aloud God's Word in 1 John 4:18 until you believe it.

Peacock Soup

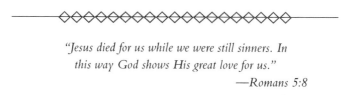

*"Jesus died for us while we were still sinners. In
this way God shows His great love for us."*
—*Romans 5:8*

The Bible says in Romans 3:23, "All people have sinned and are not good enough for God's glory." This means everyone has sinned. We have done bad things we shouldn't do, which do not please God. And John 3:16 says, "God loved the world so much that He gave His only Son. God gave His Son so that whoever believes in Him may not be lost but have eternal life." This means that if we ask Jesus to come into our hearts to help us do good things, we please God, and we can live with Him forever in heaven.

Have you ever seen a peacock? They are beautiful birds with long tails of bright green and blue feathers. Well, this story is about peacocks. Not just any ordinary peacocks, these peacocks were very pampered. *Pampered* means they had the best of everything a peacock would want. Their cages had expensive, soft carpet on the floor, and even the yard they lived in had the best green grass. Also, the food they ate was made especially for them.

Their owners, Farmer Pete and Mrs. Pete, really loved their peacocks. Mrs. Pete would even sing to them and cuddle them every day. Farmer Pete and Mrs. Pete loved the peacocks, and the peacocks loved them.

Well, everything was going just fine for Farmer Pete, Mrs. Pete, and their peacocks. Then one day, Mrs. Pete came into the peacocks' yard and fed them but didn't sing. She really looked sad, and then she left. Now, this really worried the peacocks, and they wondered what was wrong. So they decided that the next day, they would ask her what was wrong.

The next day, when Mrs. Pete came into the yard, she did the same thing; she fed the peacocks but didn't sing. So, Luke Peacock walked up to her and asked, "Mrs. Pete, what is the matter? You haven't sung to us in two days, and you look so sad."

Mrs. Pete turned around to him and said, "I don't want to worry you, but Farmer Pete is very sick, and he isn't getting any better."

All the peacocks gasped and were shocked. "Oh no," said Luke Peacock, "that is so sad. Is there anything we can do to help?"

Mrs. Pete paused for a moment and said, "Well, there is, but I don't know if I could ask you to do it."

Luke Peacock stood boldly and said, "It doesn't matter what it is; please let us know. You know how much we love you and Farmer Pete."

In tears, Mrs. Pete answered, "Well, the doctor said there is only one thing that can make Farmer Pete better."

Luke Peacock answered, "Tell us, please tell us."

Mrs. Pete continued, "The only thing that can make him better is peacock soup." All the peacocks looked at each other, wondering what on earth she was talking about. Mrs. Pete explained that one of the peacocks would have to give up their life. Then she could make the peacock soup, and Farmer Pete could get better.

All the peacocks were even sadder knowing that one of them had to die. They wondered which one of them would be willing to do such a brave thing.

But all of a sudden, they heard the words "I will do it." Shocked, they turned around, and from the back of the cage came a young peacock named Joe Peacock. He stood before everyone and said, "I know this is a very hard thing to do. But if it will save Farmer Pete's life, I am willing to do it. I will die so he will live." So he went with Mrs. Pete.

The peacock soup was made and given to Farmer Pete. Within a few days, Farmer Pete was all better!

What a brave thing for Joe Peacock to do. You know, it reminds me of a story in the Bible. Someone gave up their life so that everyone in the world would live. His name was Jesus Christ. When God made man, He was so happy, and they had wonderful times getting to know each other. Then evil came into the world, and He couldn't have a close relationship with man anymore. This made God very sad. He wondered what He would do so that He could have a good relationship with man again.

He said, "I know, because the payment for sin is death, I can ask My Son Jesus if He would die so man can live with Me in heaven forever."

And you know what Jesus did? He said, "Yes, I will do it."

Jesus was very brave. He loves us so much that He came to earth as a baby. He grew up and then tried to teach man about how much He and God loved them. But some people didn't like it; they kept sinning and decided they would kill Jesus. So Jesus died on the cross, and when He did, He took on all the sins of the world Himself. But he didn't stay in the grave; He arose on the third day. This made it possible for all men, if they believed in Him, to have their sins forgiven. Then they could live with Jesus forever in heaven when they died. Romans 6:23

says, "The payment for sin is death. But God gives us the free gift of life forever in Christ Jesus our Lord."

Jesus gave His life so we could live in heaven with Him forever. Have you ever given up something you love so that someone you love could be happy? If not, would you be willing to?

Jesus Loves Little Children

*"Jesus took the children in his arms. He put
his hands on them and blessed them."*
—Mark 10:16

Have you heard of this song before? The words are:

> Jesus loves the little children,
> All the children of the world.
> Red and yellow, black, and white,
> They are precious in His sight.
> Jesus loves the little children of the world.

This is a song I used to sing when I was a little girl. It expresses the love Jesus has for children. Children are important to Jesus. The Bible says grown-ups should be like little children.

I want to tell you a story about Jesus and some little children. It happened a long time ago in Bible days.

Jesus went all over the country speaking to people about God's love. He healed and blessed them. Some mothers heard that Jesus was coming to where they lived in Judea. So they decided to take their children to see Jesus so He could bless them.

The mothers called their children together and told them that tomorrow, they were going to see Jesus.

"Who is Jesus?" a little one asked.

Her mother replied, "He is a holy man, and some say He is the Son of God. He heals people, blesses them, and tells them about God's love."

Another girl shouted, "I want to go see Him!"

So the mothers explained to the children that they would have to get a good night's sleep because it was going to be a long walk.

The next morning, the children were up early. They ate their breakfast, did all their chores, and put on their best clothes. They were all excited to see Jesus.

The mothers and the children started out walking. Remember, in those days, they didn't have motorbikes or cars. As they walked, people could hear the children laughing in excitement. They were on their way to see Jesus. They made so much noise and asked so many questions.

"I wonder what He looks like?" asked one girl.

"I heard He is very handsome," answered another girl.

One of the boys said, "I heard He is a very strong man."

Another boy added, "It doesn't matter to me what He looks like. I just want to see Him."

There were giggles, laughter, and excitement. When they got closer to Jesus, one of His helpers, who was called a *disciple*, came over to them and told them to be quiet. The group of mothers, boys, and girls quieted down for a moment, but they were so excited they started making noise again.

Then another disciple came over to them and said, "Were you not told to be quiet? Can't you see Jesus is speaking to the people? You are disturbing Him."

He was so disgusted he walked over to Jesus and said, "Master, I am so sorry that those children are disturbing You with all that noise. Do You want me to send them away?"

Jesus turned around and saw the group of mothers and children and said, "Let the little children come to Me. Don't stop them, because the kingdom of heaven belongs to people who are like these children."

My goodness, the children were so excited they ran over to Jesus. Some of them hugged Him, and some were even able to sit on His lap. Then Jesus blessed them.

You know, this is not a story that I just made up; it is a story in the Bible, found in Matthew 19:13–15. Jesus really loves little children.

There is another scripture in the Bible, Matthew 18:1–4, that says, "At that time the followers came to Jesus and asked, 'Who is greatest in the kingdom of heaven?' Jesus called a little child to Him. He stood the child before the followers. Then He said, 'I tell you the truth. You must change and become like little children. If you don't do this, you will never enter the kingdom of heaven. The greatest person in the kingdom of heaven is the one who makes himself humble like this child.'"

You see, Jesus wanted grown-ups to be like little children. And He told them that if they wanted to be great in His Kingdom, they had to be like children. That's how much Jesus loves you.

Another song I liked to sing when I was younger is this:

> Jesus loves me this I know,
> For the Bible tells me so.
> Little ones to Him belong,
> They are weak but He is strong.

Yes, Jesus loves me,
Yes, Jesus loves me,
Yes, Jesus loves me,
For the Bible tells me so.

I remember when I sang this song, it made me feel so good and excited, knowing that Jesus really loves me. I want you to always remember that Jesus loves all the little children of the world, and that includes you!

Do you have a favorite song to sing that reminds you of the love of Jesus?

Three Little Pigs

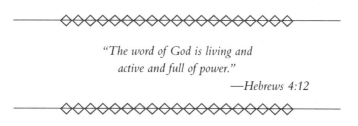

*"The word of God is living and
active and full of power."*
—*Hebrews 4:12*

When we become children of God, He gives us power to use against the devil. The devil is evil and wants to get us away from God.

The Bible says in Hebrews 4:12, "The word of God is living and powerful." The Word of God has power, so when the devil comes to hurt us, we have to pray the Word of God. If we believe the Word, we will always defeat him. Let's consider a story about three little pigs. One of them did this very same thing.

I know you have heard of the three little pigs, but the ones I am talking about are really different. These pigs were girl triplets, which means they were all born on the same day. Their parents decided to name them Susie One, Susie Two, and Susie Three. They all lived in their own homes.

Susie One had a beautiful voice. She loved singing to the Lord. She loved to worship and praise Him. She really enjoyed spending her time letting God know how much she loved and appreciated Him.

Susie Two loved to pray. She would pray all the time. She prayed when she woke up in the morning. She prayed all through the day and even before she went to bed. She enjoyed praying and thanking God and talking to Him.

Susie Three loved to read the Word of God, which is the Bible. She read all the time. She loved how the Word of God helped her be strong.

But you know, there was one person who didn't like what these three little pigs were doing. Do you know who that might be? Yes, you are absolutely right. It was the devil. The devil doesn't like anything that pleases God, so he wasn't happy at all.

He thought, *Now, I don't like anyone pleasing God, so I've got to find a way to stop these pigs.* Then suddenly, he said, "I know I will stop them one by one. For Susie One, I will send Pride to stop her in her tracks. She won't be singing many praises to God after that."

Pride means you think everything is about you and you don't need anybody else to tell you what to do. So Pride came and knocked on Susie One's door.

"Who is it?" she asked.

"It's only me," Pride answered.

"What do you want?" Susie One asked.

"Oh, I just want to talk to you for a moment," replied Pride.

So Susie One got up and opened the door. Immediately Pride started to tell her how she had such a beautiful voice and how everybody loved it. He told her people thought she sang like Beyonce and she should make some records. He told her it wouldn't be about singing to only God, but she could be making a lot of money.

Susie One thought for a moment. Then she said, "You know, you are absolutely right. I do have a beautiful voice, and people should hear me sing. My voice is fabulous, and Beyonce can't be compared to me. I am a great singer."

Then Susie One got so excited about trying to make money she forgot about praising and worshipping God.

When the devil saw this, he was so excited and said, "Great job, Pride. Now, let me see what I can do to stop Susie Two." He came up with the idea of sending Busy to Susie Two.

Busy came to Susie Two's door and knocked.

"Who is it?" she asked.

Busy answered, "Oh, it's just me, Busy. Can I come in?"

"What do you want?" she asked.

"I just want to talk to you for a moment," he replied.

Susie Two said, "Okay," and opened the door.

Busy began telling Susie Two about all the things she was missing out on because she prayed so much. He told her about the latest television shows, the movies, the new shops at the mall, the new video games, and so many other things.

Susie Two decided that he was absolutely right. She had never thought about how many things she was missing. She started doing so many things that she didn't have time to pray to God anymore.

The devil saw what was happening with Susie One and Susie Two. He was so excited, and he couldn't wait to stop Susie Three. Now, he had to really think hard about stopping Susie Three. You see, he knew how powerful the Word of God is. He said to himself, "I know I will send three things to her. They will definitely stop her. I will send Sickness, Doubt, and Fear."

First, Sickness knocked on Susie Three's door.

"Who is it?" she asked.

Sickness answered, "It is Sickness. Can I come in?"

"No way," said Susie Three. "The Bible says in 1 Peter 2:24, 'Christ carried our sins in His body on the cross. He did this so that we would stop living for sin and start living for what is right. And we are healed because of His wounds.' So, I am not letting you in."

Sickness left.

Then Doubt knocked on Susie Three's door.

"Who is it?" she asked.

Doubt answered, "It's Doubt. Can I come in?"

"No way," Susie Three said. "The Bible says in James 1:6–8, 'When you ask God, you must believe. Do not doubt God. Anyone who doubts is like a wave in the sea. The wind blows the wave up and down. He who doubts is thinking two different things at the same time. He cannot decide about anything he does. A person like that should not think that he will receive anything from the Lord.'" She added, "So no way am I letting you in."

Doubt left.

Now, the devil was getting mad because Sickness and Doubt didn't work. He said to himself, "I know Fear will definitely stop her. Go Fear!"

Fear knocked on Susie Three's door.

"Who is it?" she asked.

"It's me, Fear. I don't want to bother you, but can I come in and talk to you, just for a minute?" he asked in a really sweet voice. He thought this would get her to open the door to him.

Susie Three shouted to Fear and said, "Absolutely not, no way! I definitely have something to say to you, though. The Bible says in 2 Timothy 1:7 that God did not give me a spirit that makes me afraid. He gave me a spirit of power and love and self-control, so I don't want anything from you. Get away from my house now in the name of Jesus."

Fear left immediately.

Susie Three thought, *If the devil has tried to attack me, I wonder if he tried the same thing with my sisters.* She had not spoken to her sisters in a long time, so she decided to check up on them.

She first went to see Susie Two. "How are you?" she asked.

"Not so good," Susie Two answered. "I have been busy doing so many things I don't have time to pray anymore. I am so sad."

Susie Three said, "You know, God's Word says in Luke 18:1 we should always pray and never lose hope."

When Susie Two heard the Word of God, she prayed. She asked God to forgive her and to help her never lose hope. She promised to try never to be so busy that she did not have time to pray.

Then they both went to check on Susie One. "How are you doing?" they asked her.

"Not good at all," she answered. "I guess I let Pride take over and only thought about how much money I could make. Now I am not happy when I sing, and no one wants to hear my sad voice anymore. I am so miserable."

Susie Three answered, "The Bible says in Proverbs 16:18, 'Pride leads to destruction. A proud attitude brings ruin.' And also in James 1:17, it says, 'Every good and perfect gift comes from God.' This verse means that when God gives you a gift, He wants you to use it to honor Him."

Susie Three prayed, and the sisters decided that they would check on each other more often. After this experience, they realized they needed each other even more than they had thought.

Can you think of a time when you used to sing or pray to God or read the Bible without needing someone else to tell you to do it? Do you remember why you stopped? What will you do the next time either of these things happens again?

Trust God

"The Lord saved me from a lion and a bear.
He will also save me from this Philistine."

—*1 Samuel 17:37*

The Bible tells a story about David, a shepherd boy, who stood before a giant with confidence and told him in 1 Samuel 17:45–46, "You come to me using a sword, a large spear, and a small spear. But I come to you in the name of the Lord of heaven's armies. He's the God of the armies of Israel! You have spoken out against him. Today the Lord will give you to me. I'll kill you, and I'll cut off your head." And that is exactly what David was able to do because he trusted and believed in the power of God.

Have you ever seen a giant? Have you ever seen anyone ten feet tall? Have you ever been afraid of something or someone?

Well, I have been afraid. But now, when I am afraid, I remember the story about David.

David was a shepherd boy who took care of his father's sheep. He took them out in the fields every day and watched them. He made sure they were safe. David enjoyed watching his father's sheep, and sometimes, he would sing to them and play his harp. David loved God so much that he worshipped and praised God while watching the sheep. One day while he was watching the sheep, a bear came and took one of the sheep. David ran after it, struck and killed it with his sling, and took the sheep right out of its mouth. At another time, he did the same thing to a lion that tried to take one of his sheep.

There was a war going on in the country where David lived. It was a war between Israel and Philistine. His older brothers went to fight in this war. One day, David's father asked him to go take some food to his brothers. So, David finished taking care of his sheep, brought them in from the field, and went off to take the food to his brothers.

When he got there, he found his brothers and gave them the food.

David heard a lot of shouting and asked one of the soldiers what was going on. The soldier replied, "A Philistine giant named Goliath is challenging the Israelite soldiers to fight him. But no one can defeat him."

Then David said, "I can kill this giant."

The soldier looked at David and shook his head because he saw how small David was. He told David that the king would give a reward to any man who defeated the giant.

When one of David's brothers saw him talking to the soldiers, the brother became angry. He said, "You really didn't come to bring us food. You just wanted to watch the battle."

David answered, "There is nothing wrong with me wanting to come and watch the battle."

Word got back to King Saul that someone was asking about fighting Goliath. Saul wanted to meet David and sent soldiers to find him.

David said to the king, "Don't worry, King Saul. I will go and fight this Philistine giant."

King Saul looked at David and said, "You can't go and fight this giant. You are only a young boy."

David replied, "When I was watching my father's sheep, a bear and a lion came to eat my sheep, but the Lord was with me, and I killed them both. Because the Lord is with me, I can kill this giant in the same way. I am not afraid, because God is with me."

King Saul asked David to fight the giant because all the soldiers were too afraid. The king put his heavy armor on David. He put on the breastplate, a helmet, and a thick belt and gave David his sword. Because David was so small, he could not even move with all the king's armor.

David took off all the armor, and he went to fight the giant. David had the same weapon he had when he had killed the bear and the lion; he only had his slingshot. On the way to face the giant, he stopped and took up five rocks from the river.

When the giant saw David, he laughed and asked, "Do you think I am a dog that you send this puny boy with a stick to fight me?" Then the giant swore against God and said, "Come to me, and I will kill you and feed you to the wild animals."

David replied, "You come to me with a large sword, a large spear, and a small spear, but I come to you in the name of the Lord of Heaven, who is the God of the army of Israel. Because you swore against God, His power will help me fight you. I will kill you, cut off your head, and feed your body to the birds and wild animals. Then the whole world will know that there is a God in Israel. Everyone here will realize that you don't need swords or spears because the battle belongs to the Lord. He will help me to defeat you."

When the giant heard this, he became very angry and rushed toward David. Then David took one of the rocks and put it in his sling. He swung his sling around and threw it at the giant's head. The rock sunk into his skull, and the giant fell down dead. When the Philistine army saw David kill the giant, they all ran away in fear.

David defeated the giant because he believed in the power of God. It was God who was with him. The power of God helped him fight and win this battle.

We probably won't ever have to fight a Philistine giant, but sometimes, we have scary things to do. If we can remember that God is always there to help us, we can be just like David and win every time.

Deuteronomy 31:6 says, "Be strong and brave. Don't be afraid of them. Don't be frightened. The Lord your God will go with you. He will not leave you or forget you." Whenever you have to face anything that seems too big and scary, like the giant in our story, remember God is with you. It could be taking a test, going to the dentist, or having to stand in front of your class and read. Remember God promises to always be there with you, so you don't have to be afraid.

Can you think of a time when you had to do something that was very hard and you did it anyway, even though everyone around you thought you could not do it? If so, how were you able to do it? If not, when the situation happens again, what will you do?

God Can Use You

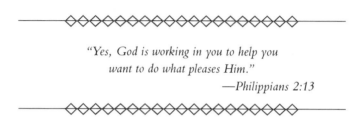

*"Yes, God is working in you to help you
want to do what pleases Him."*
—*Philippians 2:13*

God wants to help us do what pleases Him. The Bible says in 1 Thessalonians 2:4, "When we speak, we are not trying to please men. But we are trying to please God, who tests our hearts."

I want to tell you a story about a little boy in the Bible who helped Jesus perform a miracle. The Bible does not say what his name was, but in this story, I think I will name him Abiah.

Abiah lived in Galilee with his family. During this time, a man named Jesus was healing people and teaching them about the things of God. Jesus healed blind people, and they were able to see. People who could not walk were able to get up and walk because of his healing. Jesus also taught the people how to live the way God wanted them to.

Abiah had heard all these stories about Jesus, and he wanted to go see for himself. So one day, he asked his mother if he could follow the crowd who were on their way to see Jesus. Of course, his mom said yes. She packed Abiah a lunch of five loaves and two fish. She asked a neighbor if Abiah could go with him, and off they went.

When Abiah and his neighbor finally got to where Jesus was, there were many people, but they squeezed through the crowd and sat down. Abiah was so excited he could not believe he was really sitting in front of the man he had heard so much about. Some people said that Jesus was a prophet sent by God. Others said He was the son of a carpenter, and others believed He was going to be their next king. But all of that did not matter much to Abiah. He just wanted to see the man who did so many great things and taught about God and His love.

Abiah sat there and listened and saw all the wonderful things Jesus did in people's lives. He could see how much Jesus loved the people.

When lunchtime came, Abiah took out his lunch. One of Jesus's helpers said to him, "Excuse me, young man, pick up your lunch and come with me. Jesus wants to see you."

You see, when Jesus's helpers had realized it was time for lunch, they had told Jesus that the people needed to be fed. Jesus had said to go into the village and buy food for the people.

One of his helpers had answered, "But there are so many people here we don't have enough money to buy food for all of them."

It seemed like feeding all the people would be impossible, but another helper had said, "There is a young boy here that has five loaves and two fish, but I don't think that would feed all of these people."

Then Jesus had answered, "Bring him to me."

Abiah was so surprised that Jesus wanted to see him. He was excited but also a little nervous, and he thought, *Why does Jesus want to see me?*

When Jesus asked Abiah for his lunch, Abiah was so excited to be able to share his lunch with Jesus. Jesus took the five loaves and two fish and said a prayer to God. Abiah thought that Jesus was just saying grace. He did not know a miracle was about to happen.

A few minutes later, Jesus's helpers had enough bread and fish to feed all the five thousand people, including women and children. Jesus's helpers kept coming back over and over again. Each time, there were enough loaves and fish for all the people. Abiah could not believe it. He had come to see Jesus do wonderful things for other people but ended up helping Jesus do a wonderful thing.

This was a day that Abiah would never forget. In his village, he became known as the boy who helped Jesus feed five thousand people.

What an incredible story. But just because it happened way back in Bible days, thousands of years ago, doesn't mean it can't also happen today.

Jesus can use you also, just like He used Abiah. It may not be turning five loaves and two fish into enough food to feed five thousand people. But you may have someone in your class who does not have lunch and who you can share your lunch with. Or you could help your parents put away the groceries or clean the house. When you do this, you are helping Jesus, and this pleases Him.

Philippians 2:13 says, "God is working in you to help you want to do what pleases Him."

Jesus can use anybody who is willing to please Him. Are you willing?

This story is based on John 6:1–14.

Listen to God

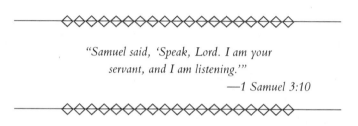

*"Samuel said, 'Speak, Lord. I am your
servant, and I am listening.'"*

—*1 Samuel 3:10*

Have you ever felt a small voice speaking to you, like someone is in your head? Well, did you know this is how God speaks to people who He loves and who love Him?

There is a story in the Bible that talks about this very thing. It is found in 1 Samuel 3.

Samuel was a young boy who served God and lived in the temple with a prophet. This prophet, named Eli, taught Samuel all about how to live a life that pleases God.

One night, when Samuel was sleeping, he heard a voice calling him. It said, "Samuel, Samuel!"

Thinking it was Eli, Samuel ran into Eli's room. "Yes, Eli, you called me?" he said.

But Eli replied, "Go back to bed. I didn't call you."

So Samuel went back to bed and fell asleep. He woke up again to a voice calling, "Samuel, Samuel!"

Samuel got up and ran into Eli's room. He answered, "Yes, Eli?"

But again, Eli replied, "Go back to bed. I didn't call you."

Samuel went back to bed and fell asleep. But he woke up again to a voice calling, "Samuel, Samuel!"

He got up and ran into Eli's room and answered, "Yes, Eli, you called me?"

Eli realized this time that God must be calling Samuel. He told Samuel to go back to his room, and when he heard the voice calling his name, he should answer, "Yes, Lord, Your servant hears You."

Sure enough, when Samuel fell asleep, the voice called, "Samuel, Samuel!"

He answered and said exactly what Eli had told him. He said, "Yes, Lord, Your servant hears You." Samuel listened to the Lord, and the Lord spoke to Him.

Wow, what an amazing story! The Lord still speaks to His people today. He speaks to us when we read the Bible, when we sing praises, when we worship Him, and when we pray to Him.

Sometimes, when we are about to make a decision that will not please God, He will speak to us. You know when you want to do things that you know are wrong and your parents told you not to do? A voice in your head is saying, "Don't do it. That is not what Mom and Dad said; you know it is wrong." Then you think about it and decide to do the right thing. Well, that is God speaking to you.

Isaiah 28:23 in the Bible says, "Listen closely to what I tell you. Listen carefully to what I say." Also, John 10:27 says, "My sheep listen to My voice. I know them, and they follow Me."

When God speaks to You, I pray you will be like the little boy, Samuel. When you hear the voice of God, you listen and say, "Here I am, God. I will obey You."

Think about the last time you were about to do something wrong. Did you hear a voice in your head speaking to you? Did you obey the voice of God?

Love Your Neighbor

*"'Love the Lord your God. Love him with
all your heart, all your soul, all your strength,
and all your mind.' Also, 'You must love
your neighbor as you love yourself.'"*
—Luke 10:27

Do you know that when you love your neighbor, you are really loving yourself? The Word of God tells us that we need to treat our neighbor as we treat ourselves. If we are mean to our neighbor, then we are actually telling them to be mean to us. So it is very important for us to treat our neighbors in the way we want to be treated.

One day, Jesus was talking to a large crowd, and He said, "Love the Lord, your God. Love Him with all your heart, all your soul, all your strength, and all your mind. Also, you must love your neighbor as you love yourself."

One man didn't understand. He asked Jesus, "Who is my neighbor?"

To help him really understand, Jesus told him this story.

One day, a man got all dressed up and packed his bags. He put them on his donkey, and off he went on a trip. Unfortunately, after a while, some robbers came and took all his belongings, including his donkey. They beat him up and left him on the side of the road bleeding and hurt.

The man was hurt and in pain. Then he heard the sounds of a donkey coming toward him. A Jewish priest was walking by. He saw the man lying there and bleeding. He quickly walked to the other side of the road and left.

After a while, the man heard the sound of someone else coming. He decided to moan a little louder, hoping they would hear him and help. It was a Levite (a man who worked in the temple). The Levite came over to see the man bleeding. But then he also quickly walked to the other side of the road.

The man lying on the road was getting weaker. He hoped someone would come by soon to help him. Then he heard the sound of a donkey coming toward him. He thought, *They probably will go by just like the others.* But suddenly, a Samaritan walked up to him and helped him up. He cleaned up his wounds and put him on the donkey.

When they got to the next town, the Samaritan went into the inn. The inn was like a hotel. He spoke to the manager. He gave the manager some money to take care of the man until he got better. The money was for a room and meals.

The Samaritan said, "If this is not enough money, I will pay the rest when I return."

Jesus finished telling the story. Then He asked, "Which one of these three men do you think was a neighbor to the man who was attacked by the robbers?"

The man answered, "The one who helped him."

Jesus said to him, "Then go and do the same thing!"

Who is your neighbor? It may be someone you know—someone who is upset or feeling bad because no one wants to play with them. It could be someone who had a bad time at home before they came to school. Jesus wants you to share His love with them. Just like the Samaritan, you could give your neighbor a hug. You could say a kind word to them, or even tell them how much Jesus loves them.

So, you see, your neighbor is anyone who needs help. Jesus wants us to share His love by helping them.

Can you think of a time when you helped your neighbor? Read Luke 10:27 again, and ask Jesus to help you be kind to your neighbors.

Jesus is the Stain Remover

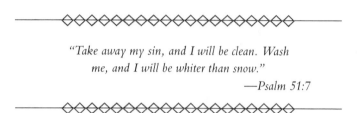

*"Take away my sin, and I will be clean. Wash
me, and I will be whiter than snow."*

—*Psalm 51:7*

Do you know what a stain remover is? You may have heard your mother
talk about getting stains out of clothes. Sometimes when you are eating
delicious chocolate ice cream, you may drop a little on your shirt. After
it rains and the ground is muddy, you may slip and fall in the mud, and
your pants get brown spots on them. When you are playing on the grass,
you may get green spots on your clothes. These spots are called *stains*.
Your mother sprays or rubs something on them to get out the spots.
What she rubs on them is called a *stain remover*.

Our clothes become really messed up and look like they need to
be thrown away. But all the chocolate ice cream, mud, and grass stains
come out when your mother uses the stain remover. She washes the
clothes, and they become clean again.

The Bible tells us about a stain remover who takes dark spots out
of our lives. The dark spots are sins that stain our hearts. They are not
chocolate ice cream, mud, or grass spots; they are the bad things we
do, like lying, cheating, stealing, disobeying, not praying to God, and
being selfish.

The Bible says in Psalm 51:7, "Take away my sin, and I will be clean. Wash me, and I will be whiter than snow." This is what King David said when the prophet Nathan told him about an awful thing he did. King David killed a man. It put a great big stain on his heart. He tried to get the stain out by trying to hide it. But the only way he could get it out was to ask God to forgive him. Through the love of God, he was forgiven, and the stain was removed.

We may try to get stains out of our lives by hiding them, but God knows and sees everything. The stains in our hearts can be removed only when we ask God to forgive us. The Bible verse 1 John 1:9 says, "If we confess our sins, He will forgive our sins. We can trust God. He does what is right. He will make us clean from all the wrongs we have done."

Jesus died on the cross for us. His love can help us get rid of all these stains. Jesus is the Stain Remover. His love helps us get rid of all the sin stains in our hearts.

Write down any stains you may have in your heart, and pray this prayer:

> "Jesus, I know You love me. I believe You can take away all the stains from my heart. Please forgive me for _____ [call out the stains you wrote down]. Thank You, Jesus, for removing all the stains from my heart. Amen!"

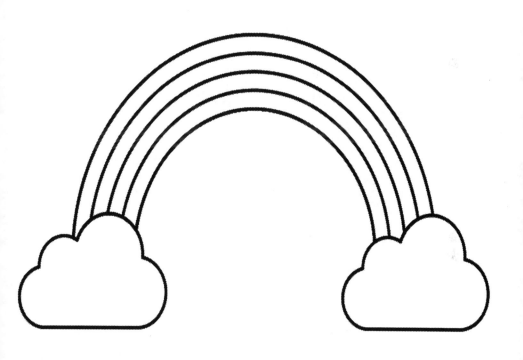

Promise Keeper

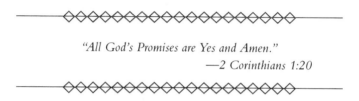

"All God's Promises are Yes and Amen."
—2 Corinthians 1:20

Do you always keep your promises? It is not always easy to keep promises. God wants us to know how important it is to keep promises that we make. When we keep our promises, it shows we can be faithful. This pleases God!

There is a story in the Bible that tells us about how God keeps His promises. It is found in Genesis 6–7. God saw that people on the earth were very wicked. They only thought of doing evil things. He was sorry He had made them. He said, "I will destroy all human beings that I made on the earth. And I will destroy every animal and everything that crawls on the earth. I will also destroy the birds of the air. This is because I am sorry that I have made them" (Genesis 6:7).

There was one man who did good things. God was pleased with him. His name was Noah. God called Noah and told him about His plan to destroy the people and the earth. God told Noah to build a large boat because He was going to send a flood to destroy everything. Noah and his family pleased God; they did everything good. God promised Noah and his family they would be able to go into the boat and be safe. He told Noah to put two of every kind of animal—a male and a female—in the boat after he finished it. He told Noah to fill the boat with plenty of food and water.

When the people saw Noah building the boat, they laughed at him and made fun of him. But Noah believed God and continued to build the boat. When he finished the boat, Noah followed God's plans and filled it with all the animals, food, and water.

Noah and his family went into the boat. All of a sudden, it started to rain very hard. It rained for forty days. The waters rose, and the boat began to float. All other people and living things on the earth died. Then God stopped the rain.

God had been faithful to His promise. Noah, his family, and all the animals were safe and came out of the boat and landed on dry land.

As Noah and his family began to thank God for keeping His promise, a rainbow appeared in the sky. God said, "I make this promise to you: I will never again destroy all living things by floodwaters. A flood will never again destroy the earth" (Genesis 9:11).

So today, anytime I see a rainbow in the sky, it reminds me that God keeps His promises.

Have you ever seen a rainbow? I have, and it is beautiful. It has pretty colors of red, orange, yellow, green, blue, and purple. These colors also remind me of how much God loves me.

Red reminds me of the blood of Jesus. He died on the cross to save us from our sins. Romans 5:8 says, "Christ died for us while we were still sinners. In this way God shows His great love for us."

Blue reminds me of Heaven. I can live with God forever in Heaven. John 3:16 says, "God loved the world so much that He gave His only Son. God gave His Son so that whoever believes in Him may not be lost but have eternal life."

Orange and yellow remind me that God wants us to be happy. The Bible says in Philippians 4:4, "Be full of joy in the Lord always, I will say again, be full of joy."

Green reminds me that Jesus gives us new life. The Bible verse 2 Corinthians 5:17 says, "If anyone belongs to Christ, then he is made new. The old things have gone; everything is made new."

Purple reminds me Jesus is our King. Revelation 17:14 says, "Jesus will defeat them, because He is Lord of lords and King of kings."

I pray the next time you see a rainbow, you will remember all the promises God has given us because He loves us so much. God always keeps His promise; He is faithful! He is the Promise Keeper!

Can you remember a time when you did not keep your promise? Perhaps you made one already this week. If you did, ask God to help you keep your promise to show that you can be faithful.

Guilt Gut

"If we confess our sins, he will forgive our sins.
We can trust God. He does what is right."

—1 John 1:9

It is not easy to confess or say when we are wrong. The devil wants us to do wrong. He makes us feel really bad, which makes it hard to confess. God is loving and is always ready to forgive us when we confess. But we have to let Him know how sorry we are and ask for forgiveness. God's forgiveness makes us feel loved and happy.

Have you ever heard of *guilt gut?* Well, I have. Some years ago, I learned about guilt gut when I was watching a television show. Let me tell you about it.

There were two children, a boy and a girl. Let's call them Nicholas and Valerie. Well, one day, Nicholas and Valerie decided to go to their neighbor's house and take some apples off his tree without asking. We all know that's stealing, right?

The next day, they felt really bad about it, which means they felt guilty. Strangely enough, with that guilt, Nicholas and Valerie developed the awful habit of belching. The more they thought about it, the more they belched. They were so upset.

They went to Uncle Lewis to find out how they could stop belching. When they walked up to Uncle Lewis, all he heard was belching. "What is all of this?" he asked them.

Nicholas answered, "We don't know, and we don't know how to stop."

Valerie nodded.

Uncle Lewis asked, "When did it start?"

Nicholas and Valerie looked at each other. They were not sure what to say. They didn't want Uncle Lewis to know they had stolen the neighbor's apples.

Nicholas replied, "It started yesterday afternoon. We think it is because we may have done something wrong."

Now, Nicholas and Valerie did not know the neighbor had talked to Uncle Lewis that morning. The neighbor had told Uncle Lewis that he knew Nicholas and Valerie stole his apples. So Uncle Lewis decided that he would teach them a lesson. He told Nicholas and Valerie they had guilt gut.

"Guilt gut," both Nicholas and Valerie replied. "What's that?" they asked.

"Well," Uncle Lewis said, "it is a feeling you get in your stomach when you do something you are not supposed to, especially when you know it is wrong. And it makes you belch like crazy."

"Oh!" they replied together. "But how do we get rid of it?"

Uncle Lewis said, "You have to do some nice things for other people. Then it should stop."

Nicholas and Valerie were so excited to get rid of their guilt gut. They quickly ran off to do some nice things for other people. They really worked hard over the next few days. They cleaned out the garage for Dad, they took out the trash for Mom, but the guilt gut still didn't go away. So they decided maybe they had not done enough nice things. They cleaned their rooms for Mom. They washed and dried the dishes for their sister. They also raked up the leaves in the yard for their brother.

But you know, the guilt gut still didn't go away. They were so tired after doing so many nice things but thought they still should more. That night, all they wanted to do was get a bath and go to bed. They hoped by the next morning, the guilt gut would be gone. But when they woke up, the guilt gut was still there.

They decided they had to go talk to Uncle Lewis again. They told him of all the nice things they had done and said they could not understand why the guilt gut hadn't gone away.

"Well," Uncle Lewis said, "you still have guilt gut because you are still guilty."

"What?" they answered. "You mean, after all the nice things we did, we are still guilty?"

"Yes," Uncle Lewis answered. "You did all those nice things, but you forgot about the bad thing you did. Remember, you did steal apples from the neighbor's tree."

Nicholas and Valerie looked at each other in shock. They didn't think Uncle Lewis knew about the stolen apples.

Uncle Lewis continued, "The Bible says in Psalm 38:18, 'If I do not confess my guilt, I am troubled by my sin.' This means that when we sin, we feel guilty about it. We have to admit to the wrong that we have done. You and Valerie haven't done that. Also, do you know that when we admit to what we have done wrong and tell Jesus how sorry we are, He will forgive us? And 1 John 1:9 says, 'If we confess our sins, He will forgive our sins. We can trust God. He does what is right.' And then the guilt gut goes away. Now, are you two ready to confess your sin to Jesus?"

"Yes," they answered.

Uncle Lewis prayed with them. But they still had one more thing to do. Do you know what it might be? Yes, they had to go tell the neighbor what they had done and ask him to forgive them.

Now that you know what guilt gut is, I want you to remember that when you do bad things and that feeling comes up in your stomach, you have to confess your sin to Jesus. Then He can forgive you. He will give you the strength to admit you were wrong and ask for forgiveness.

Write down the steps that Nicholas and Valerie had to take to get rid of guilt gut. Put them up on your wall for you to use the next time you may have to confess and say you are sorry.

God's Golden Rule

*"Do for other people the same things you want
them to do for you. This is the meaning of the
law of Moses and the teaching of the prophets."*
—Matthew 7:12

God's Golden Rule has been around for a long time. This verse tells us that it was around in the time Moses lived on the earth. But it seems today, so many people forget it or don't use it. Maybe this is the reason why so many people are unhappy. If we want to be happy and loved, then we have to treat others with kindness and with love.

Macy and her mom had just moved to Holly Valley. It was Macy's first day of school. She was a little bit nervous but still excited about her new school. She was hoping to meet some new friends. She got dressed, looked in the mirror, and shrugged her shoulders. Her clothes were old, but she knew her mom was having a rough time after Dad had gone to Heaven.

Macy went downstairs. In her excitement, she gobbled down her food, ran out the door, and jumped into the car.

When they arrived at the school, Macy kissed Mom goodbye. Mom asked her, "Are you sure you don't want me to go in with you?"

"No," Macy answered, but Mom followed her in anyway, just in case.

The principal met Mom and Macy and introduced herself. She said to Mom, "It's okay. I can take her to class." Then Mom left.

When the principal and Macy reached the class, Macy was introduced to her teacher, Miss Blackwell. Macy thought Miss Blackwell was pretty and very nice. Miss Blackwell introduced Macy to the class and took her to her seat. Macy really enjoyed her first day at school. The work wasn't hard at all.

After a few weeks, she was still enjoying herself for the most part. She had made only one new friend. Her friend's name was Brandy. She was very nice to Macy. They spent every break together and began to spend time at each other's homes.

After a few months, everyone in Macy's class received invitations to Sasha's birthday party. Sasha was the popular girl who everyone loved, and she made sure everyone knew it. She would make fun of what Macy wore to school sometimes. She would get the other kids to laugh at Macy.

When Sasha gave Macy her invitation, she said, "My mother said I have to invite everyone, so here." It really didn't bother Macy; she was just so excited that she was going to a party.

When Macy got home, she told Mom all about it. She said, "But Mom, I don't have anything to wear. I know we don't have any money for a gift, so maybe I should not go."

Mom looked at Macy and said, "Well, don't worry. It doesn't matter what you wear. Also, you can paint her a picture as a gift." You see, Macy was a very good artist, and her paintings were very beautiful. Many people loved her paintings. Mom continued, "And besides, I can get one of your best dresses, clean it up, and iron it. It will be fine."

Macy started on Sasha's birthday present right away.

Well, it was soon the day of Sasha's party, and Macy was so excited. She got dressed and carefully wrapped Sasha's gift. Brandy and her mom came to pick up Macy.

When they arrived, everyone else was already there. Most of the girls were with Sasha when she made a nasty comment about Macy's dress. They laughed, of course, until Sasha's mom stopped them. She went over to Macy and hugged her, which made Macy feel better.

Macy was having fun with Brandy. Then it came time for Sasha to open her presents. She opened all her gifts besides one; it was Macy's. Sasha's mom passed it to her, but she said she would open it later. She whispered to one of her friends that she didn't want to be embarrassed by what might be in it. This hurt Macy's feelings.

At school the next day, Sasha came up to Macy and said, "Hello," with a big smile on her face.

Macy was surprised but accepted it and thought, *Wow, I wonder what happened for her to do that. She has never been nice to me.*

Everyone else was surprised too! Well, during break, Sasha asked Macy if she could talk to her alone. Sasha looked at Macy and started to cry. Macy asked, "What's the matter, Sasha?"

Sasha wiped her eyes and blurted out, "I am so sorry, Macy, for how I have been treating you. Can you forgive me?"

In shock, Macy answered, "Sure, of course."

Sasha explained, "When I opened your gift, I saw the beautiful picture you painted for me. I couldn't believe how great it was. You are a very good artist. When my Mom saw it, we were both shocked. I started to cry, and Mom asked what was wrong. I told her that I felt so awful because I was treating you so bad. When you first came to school, you were not dressed nice, and sometimes, your hair was messy. I thought, *This girl is so poor. I don't want to have anything to do with her.* So I treated you badly. Each time everyone laughed made me feel good! That's when Mom reminded me about a story we learned in Sunday school about God's Golden Rule."

Macy interrupted, "What story is that?"

Sasha continued, "It is found in the Bible in Matthew 7:12. It says, 'Do for other people the same things you want them to do for you.' It means I have to treat people the way I want to be treated. I didn't treat you in a good way. Now, I know how much it must have hurt you. I am so sorry. I would not want you to treat me the way I treated you."

Macy turned to Sasha and said, "It's okay. I forgive you."

This is a golden rule, and it is so important. If you are treating other people in a bad way, it means you must want them to treat you in a bad way also. But if you want people to be kind and loving to you, then you have to be kind and loving to them.

Think of someone you may have been mean to. Ask God to give you the courage to ask for their forgiveness. Then make a note of how you can make it up to them.

Share God's Love

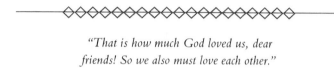

"That is how much God loved us, dear friends! So we also must love each other."

—1 John 4:11

Do you love God? Would you like to make Him happy? This verse tells us that we must love each other. This makes God happy. Sharing God's love is not always easy, but 1 John 4:7–8 says, "Dear friends, we should love each other, because love comes from God. The person who loves has become God's child and knows God. Whoever does not love does not know God, because God is love." So if we say we love God, we must love others.

Tanya was sitting on the porch in the swing, waiting for Aunt Jessie to come. She loved her aunty. She was always so happy and doing so many good things for other people, especially for her favorite niece, as Tanya considered herself to be. She was so excited. She waited right there for her aunt to arrive.

She wondered why her aunty was so happy and did so many nice things for other people. Sometimes, it even surprised Tanya, like a few weeks ago, when Tanya and Aunt Jessie had gone out for a walk. They were going to get treats from the ice-cream truck in the park. They came across this awful smell. Tanya thought, *What on earth is that? It really stinks.* To her surprise, it was a homeless man sitting on a bench. What surprised her even more was Aunt Jessie went and sat down beside him. She gave him a hug and asked if she could help him.

The man replied, "Really—you want to help me? Okay, do you have any food, because I am really hungry. I haven't eaten for a few days."

Tanya waited to see what Aunt Jessie was going to do. Immediately, Aunt Jessie said, "Wait here. I will be right back."

Aunt Jessie took Tanya's hand, and off they went. They passed the ice-cream truck, which didn't make Tanya happy at all. They ended up at the corner store. There, Aunt Jessie bought some food for the homeless man. Then they went back to the park.

Before Aunt Jessie gave him the food, she asked if she could pray for him. The man agreed. So Aunt Jessie prayed for him, then gave him the food. He was so grateful he began to cry. Aunt Jessie told him, "Don't cry. God brought me here today just to bless you. He loves and cares for you, and so do I." Then she gave him a great big hug.

As they walked away, Tanya could not understand why her aunt would do such a thing.

Just last week at the grocery store, as Tanya and Aunt Jessie were walking in, Miss Grouchy Pouchy pushed past them in a hurry on her way out. She shouted, "Get out of my way!"

Miss Grouchy Pouchy wasn't really her name. Her real name was Miss Jones. Everyone called her that because she was so grouchy and mean. She pushed past them and dropped all her shopping bags.

Aunt Jessie moved to the side and replied with a smile, "Oh, I am so sorry. Please forgive me." She picked up all the bags and gave them to Miss Jones, who was very surprised because usually, people just ignored her. But there was something different about Aunt Jessie, and Miss Jones even smiled at her.

After helping Miss Jones with her bags, Aunt Jessie asked, "Can I help you carry them to your car?"

Miss Jones was shocked. She stopped for a moment, then said, "Why, yes, you can. Thank you."

Tanya couldn't believe Aunt Jessie was helping Miss Grouchy Pouchy. Also, Miss Grouchy Pouchy was actually being nice. She even smiled, which was very, very surprising. This was the sort of thing Aunt Jessie always did. Today, Tanya decided to ask her why, because she really didn't understand it at all.

When Aunt Jessie finally arrived, Tanya ran to her and gave her a big hug and lots of kisses. She said, "Aunt Jessie, before you go into the house, can I talk to you for a moment?"

Aunt Jessie replied, "Of course."

Tanya said, "I don't understand why you always do so many nice things for people you don't even know. You are always so happy and smiling all the time. You are always singing and being so joyful, and I want to know why."

Aunt Jessie answered, "The Bible says in 1 John 4:7–11, 'Dear friends, we should love each other, because love comes from God. The person who loves has become God's child and knows God. Whoever does not love does not know God, because God is love. This is how God showed His love to us: He sent His only Son into the world to give us life through Him. True love is God's love for us, not our love for God. God sent His Son to die in our place to take away our sins. That is how much God loved us, dear friends! So we also must love each other.'"

She continued, "I know God loves me, and I want to show how much I love Him. This verse tells me I must love others, and this makes me so happy. When I wake up every morning, I ask God to help me show His love to everyone I meet. This makes God happy, so it makes me happy too!"

If you love God and want to make Him happy, make a list of some things you can do to show God's love. Perhaps you can make someone in your class happy when you go back to school.

Stress Under The Christmas Tree

"Peter began to speak: 'I really understand now
that to God every person is the same.'"

—*Acts 10:34*

It was Christmas Eve, and all the family had gone to sleep. Well, now it was a quiet, peaceful night, but earlier, the house had been filled with excitement as Karen couldn't sleep. She couldn't wait to see what would be under the tree on Christmas morning.

All was quiet when suddenly, under the tree, someone could be heard saying, "Oh my goodness, I don't believe it. You have got to be kidding me, for real!"

The noise was loud and was coming from the tea set. Well, it startled the paint set as he tried to shoosh the Tea Set.

"Are you crazy? Do you want to wake up everyone in the house? Be quiet!" Paint Set said.

"Be quiet?" Tea Set asked. "I am sorry, but I can't believe what I am seeing."

"What are you talking about?" asked Paint Set.

Tea Set replied, "It is unbelievable! Really! Shut my mouth?"

Getting irritated now, Paint Set demanded she tell him what was wrong. Tea Set calmed down a little and said, "Can't you see that over there? What's wrong with you?"

Being even more irritated, Paint Set asked, "What? I don't see anything unusual over there."

Tea Set replied, "Are you blind? See, that teddy bear over there!"

"And so what?" replied Paint Set. "He is a Christmas gift for Karen, just like we are."

"But he is a teddy bear," Tea Set retorted.

"Yes, I can see that. He looks very handsome with that bright red bow tie," answered Paint Set.

"Ugh," shuttered Tea Set, "you don't understand."

"So explain it to me," replied Paint Set, getting even more irritated.

"Well," said Tea Set, "yes, we are all Christmas gifts for Karen, but he is a teddy bear. Teddy bears are cute, cuddly, and become good friends with you, but we are just regular toys. Karen will play with me and have fun, but eventually, I will wear away. I may even get chipped or broken, and that's the end of me. And with you, she will paint and have fun. Eventually, you may dry up, and she will no longer have any interest in you."

"Oh, now I see," replied Paint Set. Then he, too, became distressed and said, "Oh my goodness, this is awful," getting even more stressed out!

But did you know there is a scripture in the Bible that could have helped Tea Set and Paint Set? It would have helped them understand that they were just as important to Karen as a teddy bear. It says, "Now, in Christ, there is no difference between Jew and Greek. There is no difference between slaves and free men. There is no difference between male and female. You are all the same in Christ Jesus" (Galatians 3:28).

God doesn't have favorites. When we ask Jesus to come into our hearts, God accepts us just the way we are. Tea Set and Paint Set could have realized they were just as important to Karen as Teddy Bear.

You see, Karen played with Tea Set and had a lot of fun. She asked Mommy and Daddy to play with her. She had fun serving them tea and biscuits. Through this fun experience, God used Tea Set to teach Karen to love her parents even more, and also to find the joy in serving others.

Karen played with Paint Set many times too. She used Paint Set to draw and paint beautiful pictures. One day, she was painting a tree in her backyard when she noticed how beautiful the trees, flowers, birds, bees, and butterflies were. Karen even took a moment to pray to God and thanked Him for His beautiful creation. Paint Set helped Karen understand the beauty of God's creation.

God has a plan for each of us. In Jeremiah 29:11, the Lord says, "'I say this because I know what I have planned for you. ... I have good plans for you. I don't plan to hurt you. I have plans to give you hope and a good future.'" God has a plan for you too.

The Bible verse 1 Corinthians 12:4–6 says, "There are different kinds of gifts; but they are all from the same Spirit. There are different ways to serve; but all these ways are from the same Lord. And there are different ways that God works in people; but all these ways are from the same God. God works in us all in everything we do."

So don't be upset if you are not able to pray like Elder John or you are not able to read the Bible like Deacon Roy. God has a work for even you to do. You may be young, but it doesn't matter.

In the Bible, Paul tells a young man named Timothy in 1 Timothy 4:12, "You are young, but do not let anyone treat you as if you were not important. Be an example to show the believers how they should live. Show them with your words, with the way you live, with your love, with your faith, and with your pure life."

God doesn't have favorites! He can use you too. When you are in school, you can be obedient to your teachers. They will notice your good behavior and be proud of you. Then they will see the love of God in you. The other kids may laugh when someone falls. You could help that person up. They will see how kind you are. I bet it will make them feel a lot better. If someone in your class doesn't have lunch, you can share yours. This is showing them the love of God. When a friend is upset, you could pray for them. Even if one of your friends is sick, you can pray for their healing. In all these things, God is using you to show His love.

Jesus tells us this in Matthew 5:16: "In the same way, you should be a light for other people. Live so that they will see the good things you do. Live so that they will praise your Father in heaven."

Write down at least three things you could do to show God's love to others.

Clancy The Clam

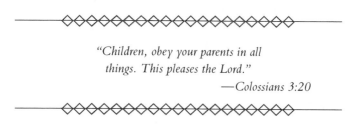

"Children, obey your parents in all
things. This pleases the Lord."
—*Colossians 3:20*

God wants us to obey our parents in all things. This is important because God gives our parents wisdom, and they know what is best for us. Not only that, but God says this will please Him.

Clancy Clam lived in the beautiful blue ocean with his father, mother, sister, and brother. They were happy living in the sand beds. The sand beds kept them safe from being caught.

Clancy Clam enjoyed his days playing in the sand with his sister and brother. They had so much fun.

One day while they were playing, Clancy saw a very shiny object and stopped to look. He was amazed at how shiny it was. He asked his sister and brother, "What is that?"

They both replied, "We don't know." They had never seen anything like this before.

The siblings decided to go ask Mother. She told them that it was very dangerous and they should never go near it. Clancy, his brother, and his sister promised to never go near it.

But a few days later, the shiny object showed up again, and Clancy thought, *It doesn't look dangerous to me. Maybe Mother didn't understand what I was talking about.* Just to be safe, he thought he would go ask his father about it.

After listening to Clancy, his father repeated the same thing Mother Clam had said: "It is very dangerous. Do not go near it."

Clancy thought, *It does not seem that bad, because it is so shiny and nice.*

A few days later, the shiny object showed up again. Clancy decided, *I've got to get closer to really see what it is.* He was all alone. He decided to check it out.

He moved closer and closer to the shiny object. But what Clancy didn't know was that the shiny object was a rake. It was used to rake up the sand to get clams. Clams were caught to be cooked in clam stew.

All of a sudden, as Clancy got closer, he was swished around in the sand. Before he knew it, he was in the hands of a man. Clancy was so frightened all he could do was cry for his father and mother. He wished he had listened to them because now, he realized he was in real trouble.

Fortunately for Clancy, a big wave came in. It knocked the man down, and Clancy fell out of his hand. The man was so shaken up by the wave he just got up and left. Clancy quickly crawled back to his home. He was so upset.

He cried out to his parents. He told them what had happened. Of course they were very upset, but they were so glad that he was okay. They reminded Clancy that it was important for him to obey them because they knew what was best for him. Clancy promised his parents that he would always try to be obedient.

The Bible says in Ephesians 6:1–4, "Children, obey your parents the way the Lord wants. This is the right thing to do. The command says, 'Honor your father and mother.' This is the first command that has a promise with it. The promise is 'Then everything will be well with you, and you will have a long life on the earth.'" God gave you this command because He loves you and wants you to be safe. His Word says, "If you obey your parents, then everything will be well with you."

Clancy didn't realize this until it was almost too late. You can learn from Clancy's mistake and obey your parents in all things.

When your parents tell you to turn off your favorite TV show and do your homework, it is important. They know that when you do your homework, you get good grades. When Mom bakes cookies, she tells you not to eat any until they cool. Mom knows if you don't let them cool down, you could burn your tongue or lips; you could also upset your stomach.

But the most important thing is when you disobey your parents, Jesus is not pleased with you. His Word says, "Children, obey your parents, and everything will go well with you."

Write a promise note to Jesus today. Tell Him how you will obey your parents so He can be pleased, and everything will be well with you!

God is a God of Miracles

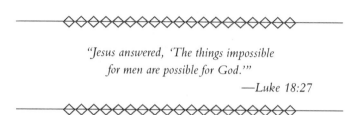

*"Jesus answered, 'The things impossible
for men are possible for God.'"*
—Luke 18:27

Sometimes, we may have some hard things to do that we feel are impossible. But God wants us to believe and trust in Him because He can do great and wonderful things.

This story is a little different because a grandson who lived in Bible days tells it. It was told to him by his grandfather. The grandson starts the story as follows:

> Hello, my name is Gomer, and I am a grandson of Noah—yes, the man who God used to build an ark. I was not born when this happened, but Grandpa told me all about it.
>
> People became very evil, and they were not following God's commands. This made God very sad that he even made man. So He decided to destroy the world with a flood and start all over again. He knew that my grandfather and his family were the only people who obeyed Him and did good things all the time. When

He told my grandpa about the ark, God also promised to save Grandpa's family. Of course, since my grandpa believed God, he started to work on the ark right away. God told him what kind of wood to use, how big the ark should be, and how to make it. This is one of the first miracles of this story because Grandpa had never even seen rain before, but he trusted God.

All the people laughed and made fun of Grandpa and his family as they continued the job of building the ark. They called them names and said Grandpa's family was crazy. But still, they continued. Grandpa said that building the ark was also a miracle because it was so big. It measured fifty cubits long, thirty cubits high, and twenty cubits wide. That is as big as a football field and as high as a three-story house. It took them over forty years to build the ark.

Grandpa said miracle number three was when God told him to put every living creature that lived on the land on the ark. There were no fights between the animals. The animals did not try to eat each other. They lived in peace on the ark.

As soon as the animals were on the ark, God sealed the door, and it started to rain. Grandpa was sad, though. He had tried to get the people to stop doing evil things and turn back to God. They had ignored him, and they all died in the flood.

Miracle number four was it rained for forty days and forty nights. Grandpa; Grandma; their sons, Japheth, Shem, and Ham, along with their wives; and all the animals were safe. Finally, the rain stopped. They did not get off the ark, because they had to wait for the land to dry up. The ark landed on a mountain called Mount Ararat.

Eventually, Grandpa's family opened the door, and all the animals left the ark. Do you know the first thing Grandpa did when the family came off? No, he did not kiss the ground and get all excited because they were safe. He made an altar and burned an offering of thanks to God. This was his way of praising and thanking God for keeping all of them, including the animals, safe.

Just as he finished giving thanks, miracle number five happened. God placed a beautiful rainbow in the sky. When Grandpa asked God about it, God said, "In the future, when you see a rainbow in the sky, it will remind you of my promise that I will never destroy the earth again with water."

So Grandpa Noah and his family lived on the earth. They continued to follow God's commands, and He blessed them.

In this story, recorded in Genesis chapters 6–8, we have learned that God is able to do wonderful things in our lives when we believe and trust Him. Take a few minutes to think about something you want God to do in your life. Then just like Japheth's grandpa Noah, if you trust God, He will do it for you because He is a God of miracles!

The Gift of Love

"God loved the world so much that he gave his only Son. God gave his Son so that whoever believes in him may not be lost, but have eternal life."
—*John 3:16*

God showed His love for us when He sent Jesus to earth as a baby. Jesus grew up and then died for our sins so we could live with Him in heaven forever.

Children of God celebrate Jesus's birthday at Christmas. It is a time when we like to give and receive gifts. But Jesus is the most precious and best gift that God has given to us.

Christmas is not only a time of getting presents ourselves but also a time when we can show love to others. Now, we must remember God wants us to show love all the time, not just at Christmas.

The story of Jesus's birth is recorded in the Bible in Luke 1:26–42 and in Matthew 2:1–12.

God was not pleased with man because they continued to sin. Because of sin, they could not be friends with God anymore. But He loved them so much and wanted to be friends with them again. He sent Jesus to earth so man would know how much He loved them.

God chose a virgin named Mary to birth His Son, Jesus. She loved God with all her heart and followed all His commands. Mary was engaged to be married to a man named Joseph.

One day, an angel named Gabriel appeared to Mary. He said, "Hello, Mary! God has blessed you and is with you."

Mary did not understand and asked, "What do you mean?"

Gabriel answered, "Mary, do not worry. God is very pleased with you. He has selected you to give birth to a son. He wants you to name Him Jesus. He will be great, and He is the Son of the Most High. He will rule forever."

After hearing this, Mary asked, "But how will this happen? Don't you know I am a virgin?"

Gabriel answered, "The power of the Holy Spirit will come upon you, and the baby will be holy. He will be called the Son of God." He also said her cousin Elizabeth, who was very old and was thought to not be able to have a baby either, was six months pregnant. Gabriel encouraged Mary and added, "If God can do it for her, He can do this for you as well."

Mary believed everything Gabriel had told her and said, "I am a servant girl of the Lord. I trust Him, so let this happen to me as you say!"

When Joseph learned that Mary was pregnant, he was going to divorce her, but the angel Gabriel appeared to him. He said, "Joseph, do not be afraid to get married to Mary. The baby she is carrying is born of the Holy Spirit. She will have a son and give Him the name Jesus. He will save people from their sins." Gabriel reminded Joseph of what the prophets had said: that a virgin would give birth to a son. She would name Him Immanuel, which means "God is with us."

When Joseph woke up, he did just what Gabriel had told him and married Mary.

In those days, every person had to be counted in the land where they were born. They did not have computers, so everyone needed to be there to be counted. Joseph and Mary had to travel to Bethlehem to be taxed because that was their birthplace.

When they got to Bethlehem, Mary was about to give birth to Baby Jesus. They went to the inn, which is like a hotel. Because so many people had come to be taxed, there was no room. Joseph begged the innkeeper and told him that his wife was about to give birth to their son. The innkeeper felt sorry for them, so he told Joseph about a stable that was not too far away.

When they arrived at the stable, Joseph made room for Mary and made a bed out of hay. Later, Baby Jesus was born, and Mary laid him in a manger. This was a box that held the animals' food, but Joseph made it like a little crib for his baby. Joseph was happy that Mary and Baby Jesus were healthy and safe.

At the same time, out in the fields near Bethlehem, shepherds were caring for their sheep. They were sitting around a fire when suddenly, an angel appeared. The shepherds were afraid, but the angel said, "Don't worry. I have come to bring you good news. It will make everyone happy. Today, in Bethlehem, your Savior was born, and He is God's Son. You will find Him in an animal-feeding box with His parents."

Then a large group of angels appeared and joined the first angel. They started praising God and said, "Give glory to God in heaven and on earth. There will be peace to people who please God." Then the angels left and went back to heaven.

The shepherds said to each other, "You know, we should go to Bethlehem and see Baby Jesus." So they got up and went quickly to see the Baby Jesus.

When they arrived and saw Mary, Joseph, and the Baby Jesus, they were so excited and told Mary and Joseph what the angels had said. Mary kept these things in her heart and thought about them all the time. The shepherds then went back to their sheep, praising and thanking God.

The shepherds were not the only ones who visited Jesus. Wise men also came to visit Him. The wise men came to Bethlehem, met with the king, and asked about the Baby Jesus. They said, "We want to visit the baby that was born to be king of the Jews. While we were traveling, we saw a star in the east. The star was so bright we followed it and ended up here. Do you know where the baby is?"

When King Herod heard about this, it upset him. He was king and didn't want another king to take his throne. So in his secret meeting with the wise men, he asked them to let him know when they found Jesus. He said he wanted to worship Him too.

The wise men left and found Mary and Baby Jesus. They bowed down and worshipped Him. They gave Him expensive gifts of gold, frankincense, and myrrh. When they left, an angel warned them in a dream not to tell Herod where Baby Jesus was. King Herod wanted not to worship Jesus but to kill Him. So the wise men went back to their country by a different way.

After they left, an angel appeared to Joseph and said, "You must pack up your things right away and take your family to Egypt. King Herod is planning to kill your baby boy. You must stay in Egypt until I let you know when it is safe to return." So Joseph got up, immediately packed his things, and took Mary and Baby Jesus to Egypt.

God gave the world His most precious gift, His Son Jesus, because He loved us so much. Also, Jesus agreed to come live as a man so He could show us how God wants us to live. He gave up all that He had in heaven to come to earth. He was born in a stable with animals, and His bed was an animal-feeding box. What wonderful love God and His Son have for us.

God wants us to remember that Christmas is not just about getting the best toys or the nicest things. It is all about giving love. We may not be able to give expensive gifts, but we can show love in so many other ways. We can be extra nice to our family. Or we can be on our best behavior. We can share our toys with others. We can be obedient to our parents and teachers.

Why not just take a moment and think about other ways in which you could show love at Christmas? Then ask God to help you show His love so you remember Christmas is about sharing God's love.

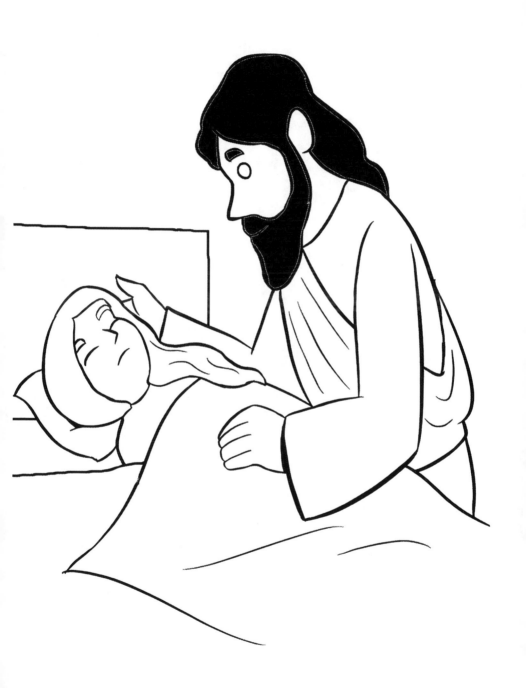

Only Believe

"When Jesus heard this, he said to Jairus, 'Don't be afraid. Just believe, and your daughter will be well.'"
—*Luke 8:50*

Being brave is not always easy, is it? Sometimes, we have some hard decisions to make or some hard things to do. God wants us to always remember that if we believe and trust Him, everything will be okay.

Our story today is about a man who did just that. Listen as his daughter tells the story, which is found in Mark 5:21–24, 35–43:

> Hello, my name is ... well, the Bible really does not give me a name. It only says that I am the daughter of a synagogue leader named Jairus. I remember my dad really enjoyed working for the Lord in the synagogue. He read scriptures, which you would call *the Bible*. He helped the people learn about the scriptures. He also helped keep the synagogue clean.
>
> I loved to go with my dad to the synagogue, but I loved playing with my friends even more. We would play with sticks or rocks or anything we could find to amuse ourselves. Sometimes, we even pretended that we were

synagogue leaders and acted like the grown-ups. It was so much fun!

One day, when I was about twelve years old, I felt sick and went into my momma's room. She felt my head and said, "You really feel hot, and you don't look so good either."

Momma gave me some medicine; then I felt a little better. I begged her to let me go out and play.

By the end of the day, I started to feel sick again. I felt even worse. She put me to bed and called a doctor.

The doctor examined me, but he could not understand why I was so sick. He gave me some medicine and told my momma, "This should make her feel better by tomorrow morning." Then the doctor left.

The next morning, I was even worse. The doctor came back and told Momma he did not understand why I was getting sicker. Sadly, he could not do anything else for me.

Each day, I got sicker and sicker. My dad had heard about a man named Jesus. He was going from town to town healing sick people. So my dad and some of his servants went to find Jesus so he could come heal me.

While my dad was looking for Jesus, I got worse and worse. My momma started to worry, but she believed Jesus would come heal me.

Days passed, but Jesus still did not come. My momma later told me about the rest of the story because after a few days, I died. She said she was so upset, and she cried and cried. She sent some servants to find my dad to let him know.

My dad finally found Jesus, and he was so excited. But the servants who my momma sent told him that I had died. They told my dad not to bother Jesus anymore.

But you know what Jesus did? He told my dad not to worry, because I was only sleeping. He said if my dad believed, then I would be well. Dad believed and came back home with Jesus.

When Jesus arrived, there were so many people crying and making so much noise. Jesus decided to just take my dad, my momma, and a few of His disciples with Him into my room.

When Jesus came in, He prayed and then took my hand and said, "Talitha cumi," which means, "Little girl, I say to you, arise." It was amazing, I heard His voice, and I got up. It felt like I had just been sleeping. I got dressed, ate some food, and then went out to play with my friends again.

Momma and Dad were so excited to have their little girl back alive. The people were shocked and praised God. My entire family, some of the servants, and neighbors saw my miracle and believed in Jesus.

Jesus told my dad not to be afraid but only to believe. He did, and he received a miracle. You may have something that is hard for you to do. Remember, if you only believe, you can receive a miracle.

The Bible says in Mark 9:23, "All things are possible for him who believes." God wants us to believe that He is all-powerful and nothing is impossible for Him to do.

Easter Celebration

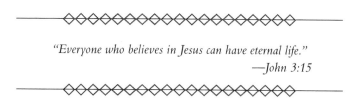

"Everyone who believes in Jesus can have eternal life."
—*John 3:15*

I know you love hunting for Easter eggs, flying kites, and playing games on the Easter holiday. I do too! But Easter celebrations are not just about all these fun things. Something wonderful happened a very long time ago for Christians. It is the reason why we celebrate Easter.

Remember at Christmastime, we celebrate Jesus's coming to earth as a baby to save His people from sin. He was God's special gift to us because He loved us so much. Jesus did what He did because He wanted us to come one day to live with Him in heaven forever. He came as a baby to show us how to live the way God wants us to live.

Jesus grew up and lived a holy life, which means He lived God's way. Jesus went from town to town and healed the sick and changed people's lives. But there were some people who did not like Jesus. They thought He came to be a king on earth. They did not like the fact that so many people loved and followed Him. These bad people decided that they would find a way to get rid of Jesus.

Then one day, as Jesus was riding into Jerusalem on a donkey, all the people praised Him. They cut branches from trees and waved them to Jesus, saying, "Hosanna to the King." The people took off their coats and laid them on the ground for Jesus to walk on. They were so excited!

Of course, the bad people were not happy, and they made a plan to get rid of Jesus. One night when Jesus was praying with His disciples in a garden called Gethsemane, they came and arrested Him. They took Jesus before a judge and told lies about him. Jesus was found guilty and was sentenced to die. Remember, this was God's plan from the beginning.

He was crucified on the cross and died. We should have died for our sins, but Jesus loved us so much that He died for us. Jesus's body was put in a grave.

On the third day, some of Jesus's friends went to the grave to pray for Him. When they got there, they could not find His body.

One of the friends, Mary, was shocked and began to cry. Then she heard a voice ask, "Woman, why are you weeping?"

She replied, "I came to pray and anoint my Lord's body, but it is missing."

The man said, "Mary."

Immediately, Mary recognized that the voice was Jesus's. Jesus told her to go tell His disciples that He was alive. Mary ran with excitement to tell the disciples and all of Jesus's friends that He was alive.

No, Easter is not just about the kite flying and game playing. Easter is about the wonderful and miraculous things Jesus did for us. He died for our sins and came back to life and went back to heaven. He is preparing a place for us. If we believe in Him when we die, we could live with Him in heaven forever.

In John 14:1–3, Jesus says, "Don't let your hearts be troubled. Trust in God. And trust in Me. There are many rooms in my Father's house.

I would not tell you this if it were not true. I am going there to prepare a place for you. After I go and prepare a place for you, I will come back. Then I will take you to be with Me so that you may be where I am."

Easter is a great and fun time, but the most wonderful thing about Easter is what Jesus did for us. The story of Jesus's death and resurrection is found in Matthew 27 and 28.

Can you think of some ways that you can celebrate and thank Jesus at Easter for what He has done for you?

Jesus Never Changes

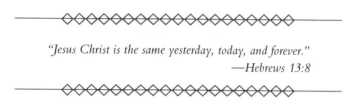

"Jesus Christ is the same yesterday, today, and forever."
—Hebrews 13:8

You may have read in the Bible about all the miracles Jesus did. Do you know Jesus still does miracles even today? He never changes! Jesus wants us to know that He can perform miracles in our lives today as well!

I want to tell you a story about a little girl named Tina. It was the last day of school before Christmas break. She was so excited and could not wait for the school bell to ring. You see, Grandma Lynn was coming to visit for Christmas.

Tina loved when Grandma Lynn visited at Christmastime because they had so much fun together. They would make Christmas crafts, bake, and decorate Christmas cookies. They would visit the rest home where the elderly lived. They also played Christmas games and did so many other activities. In fact, everything they did, Grandma would always make it about Christmas.

Finally, the bell rang. Tina wished her teacher and friends a merry Christmas, then ran out to the car.

When Tina and Mom got home, they went into the guestroom. They made sure it was tidy and comfortable for Grandma Lynn's visit. Tina even cleaned her room. She promised Mom she would keep it clean until Grandma's arrival, which was a week away.

After cleaning, Tina helped Mom get dinner ready. When Dad came home from work, they all sat down and had dinner.

The phone rang while they were watching the news. When Dad hung up, he told Mom and Tina he had some news to share with them. It was Grandma Lynn. She was not sure she would be coming for a Christmas visit this year. She had taken a fall and hurt her ankle. The doctor said it was just a sprain. He was concerned, though, that Grandma Lynn's ankle may take awhile to heal because of her age.

Of course, the family was upset because they really wanted Grandma to visit for Christmas. It had been a few years since her last visit. But do you know what Tina did? She remembered a lesson her Sunday school teacher had taught about miracles.

The lesson was about a blind man named Bartimaeus. It is found in the Bible in Mark 10:46–52. Bartimaeus was sitting on the road begging when he heard that Jesus was walking by. He shouted, "Jesus, Son of David, please help me!"

Many people told him to be quiet, but he shouted even louder. Bartimaeus had heard about a man named Jesus who was going from town to town healing people. And Bartimaeus really wanted to be healed. "Jesus, Son of David, please help me!" he shouted again.

Jesus heard him shout and stopped. Jesus said, "Tell that man to come to me."

Some of the people called Bartimaeus and said, "Cheer up, come on. Jesus is calling you."

Bartimaeus was so excited he got up, left all his belongings on the ground, and went to Jesus.

Jesus asked him, "What do you want me to do for you?"

Bartimaeus answered, "I want to see again."

Jesus said to him, "Go, you are healed because you believed."

Bartimaeus was able to see right away. Can you imagine how happy he must have been?

Tina remembered that the memory verse for this lesson was "Jesus is the same yesterday, today, and forever." Her teacher had taught her that even though Jesus did miracles in Bible days, He is still powerful. He continues to do miracles in our lives today.

At first, Tina was sad to hear the news about Grandma Lynn. Remembering the Sunday school lesson, however, she believed Jesus could do a miracle in Grandma Lynn's situation. Tina asked Mom and Dad to pray with her. They asked Jesus to heal Grandma Lynn's ankle quickly so she would be able to come for Christmas.

After praying, Tina called Grandma Lynn and told her about the Sunday school lesson. She shared that they all were believing that Jesus would perform a miracle.

Tina continued to believe and expect Grandma Lynn would be healed. After about a week, she received a phone call from Grandma Lynn. All Tina could hear on the other end of the line was "Hallelujah! Praise the Lord!" Grandma Lynn's ankle was healed, and she was ready to leave for the Christmas visit.

Tina was so excited. She ran and told Mom and Dad. They all prayed and gave thanks to Jesus for this wonderful miracle.

Jesus did so many miracles when He lived on earth. He healed the blind, the deaf, and sick people. He turned water into wine. He controlled the weather by calming a storm. He fed thousands of people with some bread and fish. He raised people from the dead. The wonderful thing about all of this is that Jesus continues to perform miracles today. He can perform miracles in your life too because He never changes. All you must do is believe just the way Bartimaeus believed.

Obeying His Commands

"Loving God means obeying his commands. And
God's commands are not too hard for us."

—1 John 5:3

The Bible tells us that Jesus came to earth to teach us how to live for God so we could live with Him forever. We must obey His commands. One of God's commands, in Exodus 10:15, says, "You should not steal." This does not just mean taking something from a store without paying for it or robbing a bank. No, it means taking anything that does not belong to you from someone else without their permission.

Listen to this story about Bobby, who learned exactly what "you should not steal" really means.

Bobby had a twin brother named Bruce. He and Bruce did everything together, from playing games to sometimes dressing alike. Also, Bobby and Bruce loved to color and paint pictures together.

One day, Bobby was coloring a Christmas picture in his coloring book when, suddenly, his green crayon broke into little pieces. He was a little upset and decided to try coloring with the red crayon. Unfortunately, the same thing happened to the red crayon. This upset

Bobby even more because he thought, *How can I color a Christmas picture without red and green crayons?*

He sat on the floor for a moment and wondered where he could find green and red crayons. Bobby realized that Bruce had the same crayons. He went to Bruce's room and took them.

Bobby thought, *I know I am supposed to ask Bruce, but I know he won't mind. When I am finished, I will put them back.* So he took the crayons, closed up the box, and went back to his room. But as he was coloring, the red and green crayons broke into pieces too. Bobby started crying. Not only would he not be able to finish his Christmas picture, but he was also worried about what Bruce would say.

As he cried, Bobby said, "Oh no, this is terrible. What am I going to do?" He thought for a moment and decided, *I know. I will put the broken crayons back in Bruce's box so he will think that he broke them himself.*

So Bobby put the crayons back into Bruce's box. He then went back to his room and decided to color the Christmas picture with different colors.

Later that day, Bobby overheard Bruce crying to Mom. Mom asked him what was wrong. Bruce answered, "Bobby stole my crayons, broke them, and put them back into my box. He is a thief. I can't believe he stole my crayons."

Mom asked, "Are you sure it was Bobby? Maybe one of your friends broke them."

"No," Bruce replied. "When my friends left, the crayons were not broken. Bobby was coloring earlier this morning, and no one else has been in my room. He is a thief."

Bobby listened and thought, *I am not a thief. I didn't steal them. I only used them.*

Mom called Bobby into the room and asked him if he had stolen and broken Bruce's crayons. Bobby blurted out, "No, Mom, I didn't steal them. I only used them because my red and green crayons broke. Then I used Bruce's crayons because I knew he would not mind. He has let me use them before. But then they broke too, so I just put them back."

Bruce shouted in reply, "You are a thief! You stole my crayons!"

Mom calmed both boys down. She reminded Bobby that being a thief is not just robbing a bank or taking something from a store without paying. Being a thief is taking something from someone else without asking for their permission. She said to Bobby, "You not only took your brother's crayons without asking his permission, but you also broke them and did not apologize for breaking them. And then you put them back without letting him know."

She continued, "Bobby, that is stealing and being sneaky just like a thief. Remember the Bible says we should not steal. That means you have not obeyed God's commands. Bobby, I want you to remember that the Bible also says that God's commands are not hard for us, because He wants us to obey Him.

"Now that you know that what you did really was stealing, you need to apologize, first to God, asking Him to forgive you and help you not to do it again. Secondly, you also need to apologize to Bruce and ask him to forgive you.

"Now, Bruce, you need to also remember that there is another command in the Bible God wants us to follow. It says in Ephesians 4:32, 'Be kind and loving to each other. Forgive each other just as God forgave you in Christ.'"

Bobby prayed and asked God to forgive him. Then he apologized to Bruce. Bruce forgave Bobby, and Bobby promised never to steal again.

Take a moment to think about this command. Did you ever take something that belonged to someone else without asking for their permission? Remember it is stealing, and God's command says we should not steal. If you have stolen and you want Jesus to forgive you, say this prayer:

"Dear Jesus, I am so sorry for stealing _____ [say whatever you stole]. I love You and want to follow Your commands so I can live with You forever. I am so sorry. Can You please forgive me and help me never do it again? I pray in Jesus's name. Amen."

There Can Be Miracles When You Believe

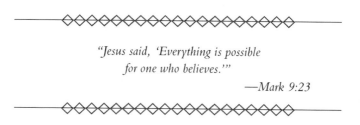

*"Jesus said, 'Everything is possible
for one who believes.'"*

—Mark 9:23

"There can be miracles when you believe." This is a lyrics in a song from the movie *The Prince of Egypt*. It is a Bible story about a boy named Joseph. He was the youngest of twelve boys. His dad made him a beautiful coat of many colors, and his brothers became jealous and bitter about it. Joseph, meanwhile, loved the Lord and spent a lot of time talking to Him.

One day, Joseph told his family members about a dream he had. In the dream, he was going to be a ruler, and they were going to worship him. His family was not impressed. His brothers became even more jealous of him. They decided to get rid of him, so they sold him as a slave to a man named Potiphar who lived in Egypt. His brothers killed a sheep and poured the blood all over Joseph's coat. They told his father that an animal had killed Joseph and dragged him away.

While in Egypt, so many bad things happened to Joseph, but he didn't forget his dream. Even when the bad things happened, Joseph still trusted God. He knew God was always with him.

After many years, Joseph's dream came true. The king of Egypt made Joseph a prince and put him in charge of all of Egypt. The Word of God says, "Everything is possible for one who believes" (Mark 9:23).

I want to tell you another story, but this story did not happen in Bible days; it happened a few years ago. It is about a boy named Charles. He lived with his mother in an apartment in the city. They didn't have much, but they were happy.

In the city where he lived and all over the world, a pandemic hit. Writer Taryn Chapman (www.parents.com) explains what a pandemic is when she writes:

> Just like a school has many classrooms, our world has many countries. One such country is China, the place where lots of people first started getting sick with COVID-19. The virus moved from person to person in China and then started making people sick all over the world.
>
> Think of a virus like a bottle of spilled glitter in your classroom. If someone has it on their hands and touches another person, then they have it on them as well. A virus is like that; if someone has it, it can get to someone else and then someone else, and so on until everyone is covered in glitter.
>
> If the kids leave the classroom, then they spread glitter to the kids all over the school. When a germ spreads to another country or across the world to many countries and gets a lot of people sick, we call that a pandemic.

Because of the pandemic, a lot of businesses and shops had to close. And that is what happened with Charles's mother; the store she worked for closed because no one was coming to buy anything. Charles's mother was very upset when she arrived home. She sat with

Charles and explained to him what had happened. She told him not to worry, because God would take care of them if they believed.

She held Charles's hands and prayed. She asked God to take care of them and to help them stay strong and believe. She reminded Charles about the Bible verse Mark 9:23: "Everything is possible to one who believes." In faith, they thanked God for taking care of them even in this tough situation.

Months went by, and Charles and his mother were really struggling. They didn't have much to eat, and so many bills had to be paid. But they continued to believe in a miracle.

One day, Charles asked his mother, "Things are getting worse, not better. Do you still think God is going to answer our prayer and give us a miracle?"

His mother replied, "Yes, I do, and we need to keep believing the Word of God." And they held hands and prayed.

A few days later, there was a knock on the door. They both looked at each other and wondered who could be at the door. When Mother opened the door, no one was there. She looked down, and there was a great big basket of food. There were fruits, pastas, meat, cookies, and so much more. Mother was so excited she called Charles to help her with the basket.

When they started to dig into the basket, a large brown envelope fell on the floor. Mother picked it up, and inside was a note and another envelope. Mom read the note. It said, "Hello, Ms. Graham. As I was praying a few days ago, the Lord told me that I needed to help you. He even told me where you lived. He also said that you had lost your job and needed a miracle. I am a businessman of many large retail stores around this city. Please accept this gift for you and your son. The money will help you pay off your bills. I would also like to offer you a job at one of my stores. Please contact me at the number on the envelope if you are interested. Also, I would like to remind you that our God is a God of miracles if we believe."

Charles and his mother were so excited. They immediately praised God and thanked Him for His goodness and their miracle.

Just like in the story of the prince of Egypt and the story of Charles and his mother, who believed in miracles, you, too, can believe in miracles. If you have prayed to God for a miracle of healing or a need, I want to remind you that there can be miracles if you just believe. Ask God to help you be strong and believe His Word, and your miracle could come true too!

Jesus

OUR GIFT

The Greatest Gift

*"God loved the world so much that he gave his only
Son. God gave his Son so that whoever believes
in him may not be lost but have eternal life."*
—John 3:16

Do you like to receive gifts? I know I do. We give gifts for birthdays, anniversaries, Easter, and Christmas; for getting good grades; and for winning a race or contest. People give gifts all the time. Gifts make people happy to receive and to give them.

But do you know what the greatest gift of all is? No, it's not that pretty dress or outfit you got for your birthday. No, it's not that awesome bike you got for Christmas. The greatest gift of all is found in John 3:16; it says, "God loved the world so much that He gave His only Son. God gave His Son so that whoever believes in Him may not be lost but have eternal life."

Yes, God's gift of salvation is the greatest gift, and He is the greatest gift giver.

The greatest gift is God's gift to the world. Because people in the world sinned, they deserved the punishment to die and not be with God in heaven. God loves people so much that He wanted to be able to live with them forever. He gave up His one and only Son, Jesus, to die on the cross for our sins. Now that Jesus took the punishment for our sins, we can live forever in heaven with Him when we die.

Now, this is the greatest gift, but how can we receive it? Another reason why this is the greatest gift is because anybody can receive it at any time. It doesn't have to be your birthday or a special occasion like Christmas.

God loves us so much He has made this available to us anytime we want to accept it. First, we must believe that Jesus is the Son of God. Then we have to ask God to forgive us for all our sins. Next, we ask Jesus to come into our hearts and help us not sin but live the way God wants us to. We have to believe in His Word and do what the Bible says we should do. Isn't this wonderful? Once we do this, we receive the greatest gift of all.

When we receive a gift for our birthday or Christmas, we can't use it and then give it away. That would really hurt the feelings of the person who gave it to us. But because God's gift of salvation is the greatest gift of all, we can share it with others.

And guess what else? This great gift never rots or wears out. It lasts forever, and it never changes. It has been around for hundreds of years and is still shared and given to people every day.

Didn't I tell you this is the greatest gift of all? Would you like to receive this great gift? Some of you may already have it. If you don't, all you have to do is pray this prayer and receive the greatest gift of all:

> "Dear Jesus, I believe You are the Son of God. I am so sorry for all the bad things I have done. I am so sorry for my sin. Can You please forgive me? I ask that You come into my heart and help me live the way God wants me to. Thank You, Jesus, for Your gift of salvation. Amen!"

That's it! You have received the greatest gift of all! Now you can share it with others!

Take a few minutes to write down the names of three people you would like to share the greatest gift of all with. Then pray and ask Jesus to help you share His gift.

The Young King

*"You are young, but do not let anyone treat you
as if you were not important. Be an example to
show the believers how they should live. Show them
with your words, with the way you live, with your
love, with your faith, and with your pure life."*
—*1 Timothy 4:12*

This verse tells us that no matter how young we are, God wants us to remember that we are still important.

This story is about a king named Josiah. His story is found in 2 Chronicles 34. When he was only eight years old, he was crowned as king of Jerusalem.

Can you imagine being a king, a queen, or even a president of a big country at eight years old? I remember when I was eight, all I wanted to do was play with my toys and friends. Being a ruler was not something I would have wanted to do. Whether you are eight or older or younger, what are some things you like to do? I am sure those do not include being the ruler of a country.

But this is just what happened to Josiah. Now, Josiah was different from the great and older kings that had ruled before him. Most of the kings had been bad kings. They did not follow God's ways. They worshipped idols and did what other gods told them to do.

When Josiah became king, a lot of people thought that he would just do what all the other kings had done. But Josiah decided to be a good king. He wanted to please God.

One of the first things he did was to follow the ways of the good king David. You remember David, the shepherd boy who fought and killed Goliath with five stones and a slingshot. He was a good king, and God was very pleased with him.

At the age of eighteen, Josiah ordered his servants to tear down and destroy all the false gods and idols, even the ones in the temple where the people worshipped. He destroyed the idols not only in his town but also in the towns all over Jerusalem.

Then Josiah decided to clean up the temple. He ordered one of his leaders to start the work of cleaning the temple in Jerusalem. One day, as the servants were cleaning the temple, they found books of rules. These books had been used years ago to teach the people how God wanted them to live. The servants showed them to the leader, who took them to Josiah.

When Josiah read the books, he felt so ashamed. He realized that the people were not living in the way God wanted them to. King Josiah talked to God and promised Him that he would follow His rules.

King Josiah gathered all the people together. He made all of them promise to accept and obey God's rules. While Josiah lived, the people obeyed the Lord.

Even though Josiah was only eight years old, the first thing he wanted to do was obey God's rules. From the ages of eight to eighteen, he concentrated on trying to teach his people how to live and obey God's rules.

You may be a member of a church but feel that because you are not a grown-up, God can't use you. But if God can use eight-year-old King Josiah, He can also use you. The Bible verse 1 Timothy 4:12 reminds us that even when we are young, God can still use us. We can show others how to live when we follow the rules in God's Word. We can be examples like Josiah.

ABOUT THE AUTHOR

Elder Marion Minors has been serving the Lord for over fifty years. She has been a pastor, Sunday School superintendent and teacher, and youth leader. She earned an associate's degree in Christian Studies from the Salvation Army College for Officers. Marion has been happily married to her husband, Ivor, for over forty-eight years and has two children and four grandchildren.

Printed in the United States
by Baker & Taylor Publisher Services